GATHERED 'ROUND

Resources for Outdoor Ministry

Kim McKellar

UNITED CHURCH PUBLISHING HOUSE
TORONTO, ONTARIO

Gathered 'Round
Resources for Outdoor Ministry

Copyright © 1997 United Church Publishing House

All rights reserved. No part of this book may be photocopied, reproduced, stored in a retrieval system, or transmitted, in any form or by any means, electronic, mechanical or otherwise without the written permission of the United Church Publishing House.

Care has been taken to trace ownership of copyright material contained in this text. The publisher will gratefully accept any information that will enable it to rectify any reference or credit in subsequent printings.

All biblical quotations, unless otherwise noted, are from the *New Revised Standard Version Bible*, copyright © 1989, by the Division of Christian Education of the National Council of the Churches of Christ in the United States of America. Used by permission.

Canadian Cataloguing in Publication Data

McKellar, Kim, 1968-
    Gathered round : resources for outdoor ministry

Includes bibliographical references.
ISBN 1-55134-075-5
1. Church camps.   2. Worship programs.   I. Title.
BV1650.M39 1997   796.54'22   C97-931244-2

United Church Publishing House
3250 Bloor Street West, Fourth Floor
Etobicoke, Ontario
Canada M8X 2Y4

416-231-5931

bookpub@uccan.org

Printed in Canada
2 3 4 5 6 7   03 02 01 00 99 98

970136

Contents

Acknowledgements 4

Foreword 5

How We Say What We Say: A Note about the Use of Images and Language 6

Part One: Theme Sessions for Faith Discovery 8
    1. Hellos 10
    2. Communication 14
    3. Trust 18
    4. Friendship 23
    5. Nature 27
    6. Faith and Faithfulness 31
    7. Promises 36
    8. Giving Thanks 39
    9. Peace 42
   10. Diversity 45
   11. Co-operation 51
   12. Goodbyes 54

Part Two: Chapel and Vespers 57
    Chapel 59
    Vespers 62

Part Three: Food for Thought: Giving Thanks 64

Part Four: Home Away from Home 70
    Covenanting Service for Camp Staff 71
    Blessing of the Bears 74
    Cabin Prayers 76

Appendix: Music 78
    Index of First Lines 101

Resource Bibliography 102

Acknowledgments

There have been many people who have shared freely their time, talent, patience and good humour in the preparation of this resource and I would like to thank especially:

Diane Ransom, Jean Ward, Suzanne Tiemstra, Jon Forbes, Jason Gallinger, and Susan Howard for all of their comments, critique, suggestions, deletions, reactions, encouragement and doodles in the margins.

Jan Bush for taking time to share her wisdom, cookies and creativity in the midst of editing her own manuscript.

Editors, Ruth Bradley St-Cyr for accepting the manuscript in the first place and Ruth Chernia for shepherding it through with patience, support, and a careful eye.

All those in graphics and print at UCPH for their creativity and attention to detail.

Campers, program staff and directors at Lake Scugog Camp, Camp Big Canoe, Sparrow Lake Camp, and Camp Simpresca. Your experience and ideas were invaluable.

My mother Charlotte for her love and encouragement; and my sister Leslie, craft owl extraordinaire, for being one of the most creative people I know and for inspiring me with endless ideas and her commitment and care for her children, their schoolmates, and friends.

And finally, Karen Baldwin, researcher, coach, and very best friend, for sharing my excitement, for telling me it could be done even when the laptop wiped the disks out, and for your love and support, thank you.

Foreword

The sound of a lone loon call across the water. A chorus of crickets singing lullabies at night. The smell of a campfire. The itch of a bug bite. Is this a house of worship? You can bet it is!

I grew up going to camp and I have been privileged in my work to travel to a number of United Church camps. I have sat on lumpy logs for chapel, been rain soaked at vespers, and sung softly into the dying embers of a campfire. And during these visits I have met many creative and dynamic leaders who find ways to bring their faith to life in a meaningful way for campers and colleagues. That is what this resource is about, and it is designed to focus on themes that are a part of everyday life—at camp or at home. I am grateful to camp staff for their willingness to share ideas and frustrations and for telling me what it is that they need in a resource. Their dedication, ingenuity, flexibility, and love for the children and youth they work with are all a part of this book.

Although this resource comes out of a camping context, I believe it can serve the church in many ways for camping programmes, youth groups, retreats, and vacation bible school. It is up to you to modify it in ways that make sense for your groups. Take this resource and use it as a springboard for your own ideas. It is meant to be out in the air, on a picnic table, in a canoe, up a tree—wherever, just not getting dusty on a library shelf.

Blessings and peace to you.

How We Say What We Say

A Note about the Use of Images and Language

One of the many gifts of camping is the diversity of the children, youth, families, and staff who come together each session. Camp is sometimes the first opportunity for children from a variety of social, economic, ethnic, and religious backgrounds to live together creating a community based on respect and acceptance. Although there may be children attending Christian camps who are active in a church congregation, there are others who are of a faith other than Christian or who have little or no religious background. An important element of church camping is the belief of the camping community in the respect, acceptance, and love for all human beings and creation. One way to show respect is by being aware of the language you use in reference to campers and other staff and also in times of worship and education.

Being aware of language really means being aware of and having respect for the people who surround you. Whether you know it or not, there will always be campers and staff from various cultures and traditions. There will be campers and staff who are a part of families that look different from your own. Stereotyping, whether racial, social, or sexual, limits how we see ourselves and others. If we are really committed to full inclusivity for adults, youth, and children, we need to realize that such inclusivity is not possible as long as the words and images that we use restrict us.

It is also a fact, and painfully so, that some children who attend camp come from home situations that are not healthy and, in fact, are places of fear and violence. We need to be aware of this when we use images of God and the church. Being intentional about incorporating a variety of images for God and humankind opens doors for people. For a child coming from a healthy home with a loving family, hearing God referred to as Father or Mother and the church called a family is probably helpful and comforting. But for a child who comes from an abusive household, it can provoke anger, fear, and sadness.

We have a responsibility as leaders—trained or untrained—to offer up a banquet of pictures, phrases, names, adjectives, and adverbs to describe our faith, our church, ourselves, and, especially, God. God is just as diverse as we are and that is something to celebrate.

Part One: Theme Sessions for Faith Discovery

This resource draws together a number of activities and ideas under one theme. But it still requires your preparation and enthusiasm. Take the time to read through the entire theme session and think about ways to adapt it to the needs of your particular group.

Each session is broken down into four basic parts: Readings, Hmmms and What Ifs?, Ideas...Ideas...Ideas, and Prayer.

Readings

The nature of camp life usually prohibits an extensive search of all relevant biblical materials to find the one perfect story to illustrate the theme of the day. The readings selected here are one or two of many stories from the Bible that fit with the chosen theme. If you know of others, use them too. The level of language and content has been adapted to make the readings more accessible to all age groups. But if the language is still too formal or difficult to understand, retell it in your own words. The point of including these readings is to show that the same issues and ideas that we deal with today were important back then.

The italicized words at the beginning of each reading section will help set the tone or context for the readings or explain situations that are unfamiliar to us.

HMMMS AND WHAT IFS?

This section could also be titled "Discussion Starters." Hmmms and What Ifs? are questions or illustrations to get you thinking and talking. Some are more suitable for younger campers, some for older campers and youth. Use your judgement in choosing which ones to use with your group. These conversations are designed for a small group setting—either with a cabin group or during a faith exploration programme. They are just a few ideas to jump start the conversation. Don't be rigid with them. If the discussion heads in an unexpected (and reasonably related) direction and the group is into it, go with the flow; or use the Hmmms and What Ifs? to bring the discussion back to close the session. You know your group better than anyone else—so use that information to facilitate a discussion that is relevant to your context and experience.

IDEAS...IDEAS...IDEAS

These are some suggestions for ways to explore the theme through music, games, and crafts. But there are thousands of other ideas that would also be suitable. If you know a craft or song that fits the theme, feel free to adapt what is included here in ways that suit your group.

PRAYER

Prayer can be a wonderful way to close a session and that is why it is found at the end of each theme section. However, it certainly can be moved ahead if that seems appropriate. These prayers are intended to be added to, altered, or changed entirely if that makes the most sense for your group. They can be led by one reader or many, said in unison or silently, sung, acted out, or used as a resource for each member to write his or her own. Prayers are ways of speaking to God and there are no limits to how and when

Hellos

READING

Deuteronomy is a book that was written to help the people of Israel to deal with a new situation. They had been slaves in Egypt, but now were on their own for the first time in centuries. God wanted them to remember what is was like for them as slaves, as strangers, a long way from home, so that the Israelites would not treat people from other countries the way they had been treated.

God wants orphans and widows to be treated fairly. God loves foreigners who live with our people and gives them food and clothing. Show love for those foreigners, for you were once foreigners in Egypt.

Adapted from Deuteronomy 10:18–19

HMMMS AND WHAT IFS

Sometimes coming to camp is like coming to a new world. We often come alone and from a distance. It can be scary and exciting and in some ways it is like the first day of school. Do you remember your first day of school? Did you know anyone else there? How did you feel? Was there anything or anyone that helped you feel included and welcome? How can we help kids feel welcome here at camp?

What are you leaving behind to be here? What do you want to get from camp? What does an inclusive community look like? How can we create that here?

IDEAS...IDEAS...IDEAS

Song:
"Ha-La-La-La" (see Appendix, page 98)

10 *Gathered 'Round*

Name Game

Invite the group to stand in a circle. One person says his or her name and at the same time performs an action such as clapping hands or making a face. The entire group repeats both the name and the action. The next person says his or her name and executes an action and the group repeats the first name and action and adds the second. And so it continues until the group is trying to remember everyone's name and action in order. One of the results of this game is that you may remember the actions of your group members instead of their names, and you will look silly as you try to call them to dinner!

Camp Bingo

Divide a sheet of paper into twelve spaces (or at least as many spaces as there are members of your group) and fill each space with a statement that might fit some of the group members. Some of the statements could be:
- someone with brothers and sisters
- freckles on their nose
- first time at camp
- someone who has a hamster

(You get the picture.) The purpose of this game is for each person to learn more about the others by finding people who match each description on the sheet. Give a copy of the sheet to each group member and ask them to find out the information and write the name of the person beside the category where they fit. You could even have an award for the person who first fills in all 12 spaces. The presentation could be held just for your group or you could link up with another group and have a party!

Memories ... memories

One of the best ways for children and youth to take home memories of camp is to make an autograph book. You might think that this activity should be kept for the final days of camp, but often there isn't enough time to get last-minute projects done, and sometimes people have to leave in the middle of a session, so what better way to start the ball rolling than by making an autograph book and having it with you for the entire time. It could even be filled in like a journal with other people adding their thoughts and ideas.

Materials
- 2 pieces of cloth, cut into 10 x 15 cm (4 x 6 in.) rectangles
- 15 to 20 pieces of paper cut slightly smaller than the material
- a hole punch
- some gimp, twine, or wool

Directions
Punch four or five holes down one of the shorter ends of the fabric and the paper. Weave gimp or twine through the holes and tie at the end. You could decorate the cover with leaves, beads, paint, or markers. Add a good pen, some new friends, and presto, instant fame.

Prayer

With each new day
God welcomes us to the world—
to new friendships or
new times with old friends,
to songs we've never sung before,
games we've never played,
colours that somehow shine more brilliantly,
water that sparkles or crashes onto shore.
God says hello in every person who we meet
every breath we take in
every sound and sight we find
in nature's path.
Welcome. Welcome to God's world.
Amen.

Communication

READINGS

God has spoken to human beings in many strange and wonderful ways. These stories tell of two different ways people hear God's voice in nature.

Moses was keeping the flock of sheep for his father-in-law, Jethro. He led his flock beyond the wilderness, and came to Horeb, the mountain of God. There the angel of God appeared to him in a flame of fire out of a bush; Moses looked, and the bush was blazing, but it was not burned up. Then Moses said, "I must stop and look at this great sight, and see why the bush is not burned up." When God saw that he had stopped to see, God called to him out of the bush, "Moses, Moses!" And he said, "Here I am."

Adapted from Exodus 3:1–5

God passed by and sent a strong wind, so strong that it was splitting mountains and breaking rocks in pieces, but God was not in the wind. The wind stopped blowing and there was an earthquake, but God was not in the earthquake. And after the earthquake there was a fire, but God was not in the fire; and after the fire there was sheer silence. When Elijah heard it, he wrapped his face in his blanket and went out and stood at the entrance of the cave. Then there came a voice to him that said, "What are you doing here, Elijah?"

Adapted from 1 Kings 19:11b–13

HMMMS AND WHAT IFS?

There are many ways that we communicate with each other. We can often learn things about people even if they haven't spoken. In what ways do we speak to each other without words? How does it feel when people do not understand us?

There are also many ways that God speaks to us. When we are loving and kind to each other, that's God speaking. When we stop to listen to the wind and the waves, we listen for the voice of God. What messages about God do we get in our world?

Have you ever heard the voice of God? Do you remember where you were? Was it loud? Was it soft? Did God use words or pictures? Have you ever tried to talk to God? What happened?

Prayer is a wonderful way to talk to God—it could be a picture prayer, a word prayer, a song, or whatever feels right. And it doesn't matter where or when, whether it's in the middle of the night or under water during swimming lessons, God always listens.

IDEAS...IDEAS..IDEAS...

Song:
"Lying in My Sleeping Bag" (see Appendix, page 84)

Zip, Zap, Pop!

This is a fun game that uses actions and nonsense words. Ask everyone to sit in a circle. One person places a hand flat on top of his or her head with fingers extended and says "zip." Whoever is sitting in the direction that the first person's fingers are pointing goes next. This person can either repeat the action of the first person or can reverse the direction by placing a hand flat under the chin with fingers pointing back in the direction of the "zip," this time saying "zap." A third option is to point at anyone in the circle and say "pop." Anyone can choose any one of these three options throughout the game. See how fast you can get the zip, zap, pops going around the circle!

Now You See It

Have you ever wanted to know the secret letter-writing techniques used by spies and secret agents around the world? Lemon writing, yes that's it, lemon writing.

Materials
- lemons or lemon juice
- cotton swabs or twigs whittled to have a dull point at one end
- white paper

Directions
Dip a swab or twig into lemon juice. Print a note on a piece of white paper. Let it dry. Exchange notes, soak the paper in water, and find the hidden message. Mysterious messages could turn up in your mailbox and now you know how to break the code. Go to it, Sherlock!

Body Prayers

One way to pray to God is to get down on your knees before bed, close your eyes, and pray. But there are many other ways to communicate with God. Try this method using no words! Break into two groups: one group will find musical instruments in the kitchen (if you have a friendly and understanding cook on site!) and the other will gather an assortment of odd items—a sheet, a candle, sneakers, and anything on the ground nearby. The "kitchen orchestra" prepares a short musical prayer, and the "flea market group" makes a still-life prayer—a picture using themselves and found items placed around them to freeze-frame into a prayer to God. But remember, no words!

A Word Prayer

*There was an announcement at
breakfast today, God.
Someone is sick and is going home.
And there was a poster up about
a flood last month. A lot of people
lost their homes and they're looking
for clothing and toys.
I listened to the loons
call out on my way
to chapel today and we sang
the greatest song.
I'm still humming it now.
The log I sat on was
old and worn smooth like glass
and the air was so wet
I could almost taste it
on my tongue.
You speak to me in so many
wonderful ways God.
Help me to hear
with my heart.
Amen.*

Trust

READINGS

In this story from the book of Matthew, Jesus has just been arrested by his enemies and now they were looking for his friends to arrest them too. Peter and Jesus were friends, but when Jesus was taken away to jail, Peter got scared and lied about knowing his friend.

Peter was sitting outside in the yard. A girl came to him and said, "You also were with Jesus." But he denied it before all of them, saying, "I do not know what you are talking about." When he went out to the porch, another girl saw him, and she said to the people standing there, "This man was with Jesus." Again Peter denied it and swore, "I do not know the man." After a little while the people came up and said to Peter, "Certainly you are also one of them, for your accent betrays you." Then he began to swear, and he swore again, "I do not know the man!" At that moment the rooster crowed. Then Peter remembered what Jesus had said: "Before the rooster crows tomorrow morning, you will deny me three times." And Peter went out and wept bitterly.

Adapted from Matthew 26:69–75

Be to me a rock of refuge, a strong fortress, to save me, for you are my rock and my fortress. Rescue me, O my God, from the hand of the wicked, from the grasp of the unjust and cruel. For you, O God, are my hope, my trust, God, from my youth.

Adapted from Psalm 71:3–5

Hmmms and What Ifs?

Jesus put his trust in Peter even though he knew that Peter would betray him. Which people in our lives do we trust? Why do we trust them? What qualities do they have that help us to trust them? Has anyone ever broken your trust? How did you feel? What does it mean to trust God? What helps us trust in God?

Ideas...Ideas...Ideas

Song:

"We are Marching" ("Siyahamba") (see Appendix, page 96)

Trust Games

When leading trust games, it is important to stress to the participants that they have the option of taking part or not. Never force participants to do something that they are uncomfortable doing. These games are fun, and for some people it can be a great way to experience trusting the group, but participation should be optional.

Trust Walk

Divide the group into pairs, one of the two blindfolded. The sighted person stands at the end of an obstacle course made up of containers, lids, and boxes, some placed close together and some far apart. The sighted person must guide each partner through the obstacle field by giving only verbal instructions. The purpose of the exercise is to steer your partner to avoid the obstacles. If one of the obstacles is hit, the partners must start over.

Trust Circle

Form a small circle of about eight people, shoulders touching, elbows bent, arms close to chest, hands at chest level, palms open and forward. One person stands in the middle of the circle with legs straight, feet together, arms crossed across the chest, and eyes closed. The person in the middle sways and falls into the circle of supportive hands, which gently pushes the middle person back into other waiting hands. In this way the person is moved around the circle experiencing what it is like to trust one's body to other people and what it is like to be supported. After a minute or two the middle person rejoins the circle and another person comes into the middle.

Will the Real Camper Please Come Out?

Sometimes trust is about seeing behind the masks that people put on to be in the world. Sometimes we pretend we are happy when we're not. Sometimes we act angry when we are really feeling sad. And that's okay ... sometimes we need those masks. The activity below is not about creating alter-egos; it is just a way of playing with the idea of who we see in the mirror and who we see in the world. And please remember to come back out!

Masks

Masks can be made with a variety of materials and, depending on the age group you are working with, some will work better than others. Here are some ideas:

Papier-mâché masks

You will need two or three consecutive sessions, at least two hours each, for this activity.

Materials
- water
- all-purpose flour
- cardboard cut into strips at least 7 cm (3 in.) wide. Length varies by head size

- newspaper ripped into long strips
- paint or other decorations

Directions

Papier-mâché paste: Add 250 mL (1 cup) of warm water gradually into 125 mL (1/2 cup) of all-purpose flour, mixing continually to prevent it from becoming lumpy.

Then
1. out of a cardboard strip, make a vertical circle to fit your face
2. stuff this cardboard frame with crumpled newspaper
3. dip newspaper strips into flour paste
4. place a layer of wet strips of newspaper over this core
5. build features out of this core using layers of paper and paste
6. allow the mask to dry for at least 24 hours, 48 hours is better
7. cut out holes for eyes and mouth
8. finish by painting or decorating

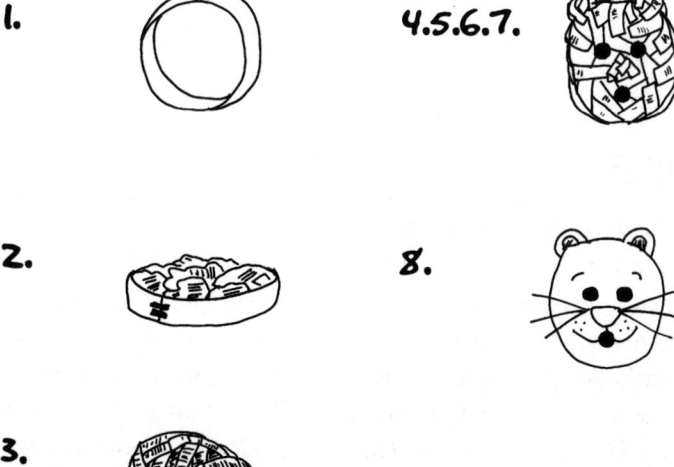

Paper bag masks
(works well with younger children)

Materials
- large paper bags
- markers, crayons, paints
- wool, material, etc.

Directions
Children place the bags over their heads to mark where their eyes are. After removing the bags, cut out spots for their eyes. Then they can design the hair, hats, and facial features from scrap materials or paint. Perhaps the group could each be a different animal or character for campfire or could use their masks in a chapel or vespers service.

Prayer

Loving God, we thank you for our time here together and we know that you are with us. God, you gave us a beautiful world to live and play in and you trust us to take care of it and each other for you. Help us to trust each other and ourselves. Help us to earn the respect of others by being gentle and honest with all your people. God, we know you are with us when we are confused about things that happen in the world and in our lives and that it is good to ask questions, and you love us even if we don't know what the answers are. We can believe in your love, God, today and always. Amen.

Friendship

READINGS

Good friends are gifts from God. Ruth and Naomi started out as strangers but became good friends. There came a time when Naomi had to leave and Ruth decided to go with her to a new land.

But Ruth said to Naomi, "Do not make me leave you or turn my back on you! Where you go, I will go; Where you live, I will live; your people shall be my people, and your God my God.

Adapted from Ruth 1:16

O God, you have searched me and known me. You know when I sit down and when I get up; you know my thoughts from far away. You watch where I am going and where I rest, and know all my ways. Even before a word is on my tongue, God, you know it completely.

Adapted from Psalm 139:1–4

HMMMS AND WHAT IFS?

Do you have friends who know you really well? What kinds of things do you like to do together? What is special about a really good friend? Is camp a friendly place? Are there people here who need a friend?

    The person who wrote Psalm 139 believed that God knew him or her completely. Just like those friends who know you so well that they can finish your sentences before you do, God knows when we are happy or angry or sad and will always stay by us.

IDEAS...IDEAS...IDEAS

Song:

"Friends" (see Appendix, page 87)

Prui

According to Andrew Fluegelman's *The New Games Book*, the Prui—pronounced PROOeee—is a "gentle friendly creature that grows." Everybody wants to be a part of the Prui. This game can be played with 10 to 50 players. Everyone stands in a group, closes their eyes and starts (carefully) milling about. Once the game is underway, the leader will whisper into the ear of one of the players making him or her the Prui. When you bump into someone, you shake hands and ask, "Prui?" If the other person asks "Prui?" back at you then you have not found the Prui.

Continue to mill about, eyes closed, asking "Prui?" to those you bump into. The Prui can walk about with open eyes to see but cannot speak, so when someone bumps into the Prui, shakes hands, and asks "Prui?" the Prui does not respond. If you find the Prui, you become part of the Prui—so open your eyes and join hands with the other Prui. You can join the Prui only at the two ends, so if you bump into two clasped hands you have to find the end. Continue until everyone is part of the gentle, friendly Prui. When everyone is joined, let out a cheer!

Rock Jewellery

This is a wonderful activity for camp. You end up with a gift to give to friends on site or take home to a friend.

Materials
- a number of pebbles/stones
- many kinds of wire of different colours and thicknesses

Directions

Have children collect pebbles and stones that are smooth, colourful, and interesting. Wrap each stone in wire. One easy way to wrap the stone is to twist part of the wire into a figure eight. Place the pebble in the centre of the figure eight and pull the loops around the stone and fasten with the loose end of the wire. To make a necklace, attach the stones to each other using wire or cord.

Friendship Twists

(This activity requires access to a supervised kitchen.) Yields approximately two dozen twists.

Materials

- 1 package (1 tablespoon) active dry yeast
- 125 mL (1/2 cup) lukewarm water
- 2 eggs, beaten
- 125 mL (1/2 cup) vegetable oil
- 250 mL (1 cup) milk
- 5 mL (1 teaspoon) salt
- 1250 mL (5 cups) all-purpose flour
- 50 mL (1/4 cup) sugar
- 1 egg, beaten
- 25 mL (2 tablespoons) coarse salt

Directions
Preheat the oven to 220° C (425° F). In a medium bowl mix together the flour, salt and sugar. Set aside. In a large bowl dissolve the yeast in the lukewarm water and whisk in the eggs, oil, and milk. Add the dry ingredients and stir to make a soft dough. Knead for 5 to 7 minutes, until the dough is smooth and shiny. Roll pieces of the dough into ropes about a 1 cm (1/2 in.) thick and 45 to 60 cm (18 to 24 in.) long.

You can form the ropes into many shapes: pretzels, hearts, birds, bugs, whatever. Place the shapes on a greased cookie sheet. Brush the tops of the shapes with the beaten egg and sprinkle the salt on top. Bake the shapes immediately for 12 to 15 minutes. Yum!

Prayer

There's something about a shared smile that makes me think of you, God. You, like the very best of friends, know what I am thinking long before I say it. Friends don't care if I swim like a stone, sing like a frog, or laugh like a crow—they love me just the way I am, the way you made me. Thank you God for all my friends, old and new. Thank you for (invite children to call out the names of their friends). Amen.

Nature

READINGS

God made the earth and God made everything that lives for a good reason.

God said, "See, I have given you all kinds of grain and all kinds of fruit for you to eat. And for all the wild animals and all the birds, and to everything that creeps on the earth, everything that has the breath of life, I have given every green plant for food." And it was so. God saw everything that God had made, and indeed, it was very good.

Adapted from Genesis 1:29–31

Consider ... a cedar tree of Lebanon, with beautiful shady branches, a tree so tall its top touches the clouds. The waters nourished it and made it grow tall, making its rivers flow around the place it was planted, sending streams to all the trees of the field. Because it was well-watered it towered high above all the trees of the field; its branches grew thick and long. All the birds in the air made their nests in its branches; under its branches all the animals of the field gave birth to their young; and in its shade all great nations lived.

Adapted from Ezekiel 31:3–6

HMMMS AND WHAT IFS?

How did you walk to your cabin or tent or to the craft hut or dining hall today? Did you follow a path or make up your own? Did you notice the ground where you walked? Was there grass, or flowers, or just sand? Whether you come from a city or town or from the country, nature is all around you. What nature is around you at home? Where is the closest tree? Is it old or young? How does the air you breathe smell?

In many ways nature is very strong and powerful but it is also fragile. We have a big impact on the world around us and have a role in taking care of the earth. What are things that we do at camp to take care of nature? What do you/can you do at home? Do you think humans have done a good job at taking care of the earth? What can we do better?

IDEAS...IDEAS...IDEAS

Song:
"The Garden Song" (see Appendix, page 78)

Nature Discovery

Materials
- Sticks, string
- Pencil, paper

Directions
Ask each child or group of children to pick out a small section of land. Use sticks and string to mark the border of it. Look at the section of ground and write down everything you see—all the plants, all the bugs, all the kinds of earth. Have the children compare lists to see the many different things in creation. Sometimes we don't take the time to look or listen to nature but when we do, look out! There's a whole big world out there just waiting to be discovered!

Leaf Stationery

Materials
- fallen leaves and bark
- paint or coloured ink pad
- white or light-coloured paper

Directions

Press a leaf or some bark into the ink pad or lightly cover it with paint. Place it onto a piece of paper. Cover the leaf or bark with scrap paper and press down firmly. Lift the scrap paper off carefully and let the print dry. Repeat as often as you like—make just one or two, or create a design out of the pattern of the leaves. This makes a great item for kids to write letters home to family or friends and it proves you actually are near trees!

Fire Cakes

Materials
- leaves, twigs, bark, pine cones, wood chips, etc. broken into small pieces
- coloured paraffin wax (old crayons work well)
- muffin tins
- paper cupcake holders

Directions

Put wax in the top of a double boiler or a can in a pot of water. Boil the water until the wax is melted. Never melt wax directly over heat! Line muffin tins with paper holders. Put bits of bark, cones, and leaves into each muffin cup. Pour wax into muffin cups until 2/3 full. Leave them to harden. At the next campfire carefully throw a couple of "cakes" into the fire ... and listen for the sounds!

Part One: *Theme Sessions* 29

Prayer

*In the bright warm glow of
prairie wheat and fireflies,
in white capped waves and
mountain snow,
in the stars, in the sun,
on the rocks, and in the soil,
we share in the beauty,
the wonder,
the strength of all that
you have created.
May we walk with care,
harvest with thanks,
and plant a promise of peace
in all that we do.
Amen.*

Faith and Faithfulness

READINGS

Having faith is a lot like having trust in someone or something. It is about believing in something even if you can't see or hear or touch it. These scriptures suggest that one way to be faithful to God, to do what God wants, and to know God is by our actions. Because we have faith, because we trust that God loves us, we show our faith by loving others. Because God treats us fairly and wants people to be kind, we then are faithful when we are kind and fair.

Jesus said, "Do for others what you would want them to do for you."

Adapted from Matthew 12:1a

And what does the Lord require of you but to do justice, to love kindness, and to walk humbly with your God?

Adapted from Micah 6:8b

HMMMS AND WHAT IFS?

The advice given in the above readings seems so simple and straightforward. But sometimes it is the simple instructions that are the most challenging to follow. How do you like to be treated? Is it easy or difficult to treat others that way?

What does it mean to do justice? to love kindness? to walk humbly with God?

Part One: *Theme Sessions* 31

IDEAS...IDEAS...IDEAS

Song:
"What Does the Lord Require?" (see Appendix, page 95)

What are some of the things we believe in even if we can't see, hear, or touch them? Love is one example. We can't put love in a bottle or smell it like a flower but we know it exists. Sometimes we create symbols to show love—we write xoxoxo at the end of a letter or draw a heart on a Valentine's Day card.

Now imagine a place where you feel safe and loved. It might be a sanctuary in a church. It might be a park or a beach. It might be your home. Picture this place in your mind and try to remember what you see—a cross? candles? banners? trees? waves? mountains? flowers? your family? your pet? a heart? a web?—whatever comes to mind is okay. If these are symbols of love and peace and kindness for you, they are also symbols of faith.

Symbols of Faith

What are some of the symbols of faith that are meaningful in your life? There are hundreds of creative ways to bring your symbols to life. Have as many supplies as you can find available and encourage campers to create a symbol or two or three of their faith or how they see themselves in God's world.

Some supplies you might want to have on hand, such as finger-paint and modelling clay, require preparation.

Finger-Paints

Materials (makes about 4 cups)
- 2 packages unflavoured gelatin
- 500 mL (2 cups) boiling water
- 250 mL (1 cup) cornstarch

- 50 mL (1/4 cup) sugar
- 500 mL (2 cups) cold water
- food colouring
- containers

Directions

Dissolve the gelatin in boiling water and set it aside. Combine the cornstarch, sugar, and cold water in a saucepan over medium heat. Stir constantly (to prevent it burning on the bottom) until mixture is thickened. Remove from the heat and add the gelatin mixture and stir well. Pour the mixture into containers and add food colouring to each.

The paints can be stored for several weeks in airtight containers in the refrigerator. This will cause them to gel. Before using the gelled paints, place the containers in hot water and stir to restore smooth consistency.

Modelling Clay

Materials
- 250 mL (1 cup) hot water
- 125 mL (1/2 cup) salt
- 250 mL (1 cup) all-purpose flour
- 25 mL (2 tablespoons) vegetable oil
- food colouring
- airtight containers

Directions

Pour hot water into a small bowl and add salt. In a large bowl, mix flour and vegetable oil and then add the salted water. When the mixture has cooled a bit, knead it until smooth. Divide the clay into portions and knead in the food colouring. Store in airtight containers.

The Faith Mobile

Materials
- coloured tissue paper or other thin paper
- wire, thin enough to bend without pliers
- gesso or white glue, thinned down with water
- 2 reasonably straight sticks
- string or wool

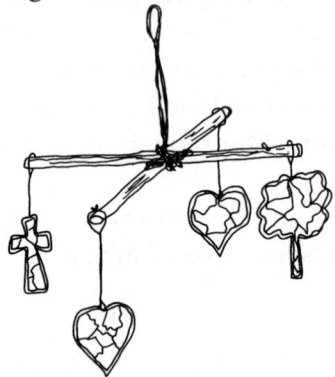

Directions

Form the wire into different shapes and symbols. Leave a loop of wire at the top of the shape to hang it up. Rip up the tissue into small pieces, coat with glue on both sides, and wrap around the wire to fill the shape. Keep adding layers of paper until the shape is completely filled on both sides. Let dry for 15 minutes. Tie the sticks together in the middle with wire or string so they form an X. Thread string or wool through the loop on the symbol and tie one end closed. Tie the other end of the string to one of the four stick ends. Try to make the strings different lengths so they will hang without hitting each other.

Prayer

When we sing in loud voices
or in whispers—
when we ask questions,
when we have doubts—
when we pray to you on our knees
or as we dance—
when we speak or act for peace and justice
when we speak or act for tenderness and truth
in our waking, in our dreaming
when we are alone or in a crowd,
with tears, with laughter,
in holding or in being held,
may we, in all things
and at all times
in your love,
live our faith in you.
Amen.

Promises

READINGS

Promises, promises! God is always making promises in the Bible and the good news is that God is also always keeping promises. The Bible word for promises is "covenant," which is an official agreement between at least two parties. One of the parties is always God and, in the Bible, it is God who starts it all. Here are two examples of promises made and promises kept. One was made to all creatures of the earth (including us!) and the other to Sarah and Abraham, who were far too old to have children of their own.

God said to Noah, "I will establish my covenant with you; and you will come into the ark: you, your sons, your wife, and your sons' wives with you. And of every living thing, all animals, you will bring two of every kind into the ark, to keep them alive with you; they shall be male and female. Every kind of bird and every kind of creeping thing of the ground, two of every kind will come into the ark, to keep them alive.

God said, "This is the sign of the covenant that I make between me and you and every living creature that is with you, for all future generations: I have set my rainbow in the clouds, and it will be a sign of the covenant between me and the earth.
    Adapted from Genesis 6:18-20 and Genesis 9:12-13

The word of God came to Abram in a vision: "Do not be afraid, Abram, I am your shield; your reward shall be very great." But Abram said, "O God, what will you give me, for I still do not have children?" God brought him outside and said, "Look toward heaven and count the stars, if you are able to count them." Then God said to him, "That is how many descendants you will have."
    Adapted from Genesis 15:1, 2, 5

HMMMS AND WHAT IFS?

Unless you like snorkelling forever, you can be glad God kept the promise to Noah! What are some of the other promises that God has made? What are some of the promises that we make at home? at camp? to our families or our friends? to God? Are there promises that people have made to us that they have not kept? How does that feel? What happens if we have broken promises to others? Are there ever promises we should not keep?

IDEAS...IDEAS...IDEAS

Song:
"Rise and Shine" (see Appendix, page 92)

Star Lights

Materials
- small tin cans, peeled and cleaned of paper (if the open top of the tin can is sharp, cover it with duct tape)
- nails
- hammer or rock
- short candles

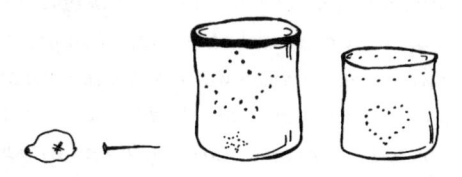

Directions
Using a hammer or rock, carefully punch holes with a nail in the sides of a tin can. Punch out the shape of a star, heart, or whatever design you would like. Put a candle in the bottom of the tin can. If it will not stand on its own, melt some wax into the bottom and stick the bottom of the

candle in the warm wax to glue it down. Light the candle and watch the stars come out shining!

Rainbow Beads

Materials (makes about 175 mL [3/4 cup])
- 75 mL (6 tablespoons) all-purpose flour
- 50 mL (1/4 cup) salt
- 50 mL (1/4 cup) cornstarch
- 50 mL (1/4 cup) warm water
- toothpicks

Directions
Mix all the ingredients together in a bowl and knead the dough until smooth and not sticky (you can add more flour if you need to). Form the dough into little balls or other shapes. Use a toothpick to make holes in the beads and leave the toothpick in the dough until it is dry so that the dough does not shrink. Allow the beads to dry for 1 to 2 days. When dry, paint the beads in a rainbow of colours and use them to make necklaces or bracelets.

Prayer

God of many colours, God of the rainbow, God of the stars ... we are reminded of the promises you have made to your people. Even when things don't turn out the way we want them to, when promises to us are broken, when we break promises we've made to each other or to ourselves, you keep your promises to us. When we are unsure of our promises, remind us to look up on a starry night and witness the blanket of love that holds your promise of love and peace. Amen.

Giving Thanks

READINGS

Psalms are a collection of poems and songs. They express strong feelings—sometimes joy, sometimes sadness. These two psalms offer thanks to God.

I will give thanks to God with my whole heart; I will tell of all your wonderful deeds. I will be glad and exult in you; I will sing praise to your name, O Most High.

Adapted from Psalm 9:1–2

Make a joyful noise to God, all the earth. Worship God with gladness; come into God's presence with singing. Know that the Lord is God. It is God that made us, and we are God's; we are God's people and the sheep of God's pasture. Enter God's gates with thanksgiving and God's courts with praise. Give thanks to God and bless God's name. For the Lord is good; God's steadfast love endures forever, and God's faithfulness to all generations.

Adapted from Psalm 100

HMMMS AND WHAT IFS?

With all those loud songs and joyful noises it sounds like giving thanks is a rowdy activity! Can you think of five things you are thankful for? How about five people? What about five reasons to thank God?

Has anyone said "thank you" to you lately? Why was it said? Was it sung? Was it yelled out loud? Sometimes we treat the words "thank you" like they are sad words. We say them very softly and quickly so that the person you are saying thank you to hardly hears them at all. Sometimes we even forget to say thank you. Do you think it would be easier to do things for others if people always said thank you? The next time someone says or does something nice for you, why not respond with a great big "thank you!" P.S. God likes "thank you's" too!

IDEAS...IDEAS...IDEAS

Song:
"Make a Joyful Noise" (see Appendix, page 90)

Group Yell
In the spirit of those loud, thankful people who wrote the psalms, try a group yell. Have the group join together in a circle or a huddle. Breathe together four times, while everyone thinks about what they are thankful for. Slowly begin to make a sound and let the sound build until it bursts into a yell. Now that's some joyful noise!

Hand to Hand
As a way to illustrate their thankfulness ask your group to make an outline of their hands on some paper. Cut the outlined hands out and write the person's name in the middle of the palm. Have them write or draw something or name someone that they are thankful for on each finger. You could offer the cut-out hands as a silent grace at your next meal or put them up in the chapel, cabin, or dining hall.

Thanksgiving Sculpture
Let the group loose for 5 to 10 minutes (indoors or outside) to find one or two things that they are thankful for. These could be fallen leaves, branches, pictures of people from home, music, a counsellor! When they come back, ask them why they chose what they did and then combine the objects

(perhaps not the counsellor) into some kind of sculpture, being careful not to damage anyone's belongings. Decorate the hall or dining area with the sculptures one night as an addition to saying or singing grace.

Celebration Central

When we celebrate people's birthdays or anniversaries, we are saying thank you for the life of that person. We celebrate the time we have known them and wish them well in the future. Why not throw a party for the camp to give thanks? You could even do a bit of investigating to find out how old the camp is and how it was born or came to be, and then invite other groups to join in the party. Bake a cake, make a card, and share your memories and good wishes about the camp.

PRAYER

You did good, God.
It was a beautiful day today. My nose was sooo cold when I woke up but then
I found your sun and I warmed right up. I did so many things today ...
I am going to hold onto today's memories like jellybeans and save them deep in my pocket for special occasions and special friends. A friend walked with me to lunch and we laughed so hard we cried. We sang my favourite song at chapel (you know, the one with the squirrel) and I painted a picture of you in arts and crafts. I hope you don't mind the purple hair.
I laughed a lot today God.
Thanks for the day.
You did good.
Amen.

Peace

READINGS

God's peace or shalom is part of God's wish for us and always has been. However, peace is not always easy to find. These two visions are both of peace—peace with creation and peace with each other.

The wolf shall live with the lamb, the leopard shall lie down with the goat and the calf and the lion and the yearling together, and a little child shall lead them. The cow and the bear shall graze, their young will lie down together; and the lion shall eat straw like the ox. The nursing child shall play over the nest of a snake, and the weaned child shall put its hand on the serpent's den. They will not hurt nor destroy anything on all my holy mountain; for the earth will be full of the knowledge of God as the waters cover the sea.

Adapted from Isaiah 11:6–9

Above all, dress yourself with love, which binds everything together in perfect harmony. And let the peace of Christ rule in your hearts, because Christ has called you in the one body. And be thankful.

Adapted from Colossians 3:14–15

HMMMS AND WHAT IFS?

Leopard and lamb, lying together? Sounds dangerous. But sometimes making peace is risky. Do you know of anyone who has taken risks for peace? What would a peaceful world be like? In order to bring about a safe and peaceful world we are told we need another kind of peace, the kind that the writer talks about in the letter to the Colossians—a peace of heart. Sometimes we have to find a place in ourselves that is quiet and at peace in order to take the steps to bring peace to the world around us. Is there a place that you go to feel close to God? Is it a physical place like under the trees or by water or can you get to it just by listening to music? Is it a place that you've imagined in your thoughts? What's it like?

There are many people in the world who live in places that are at war and they have no place to find peace around them. Maybe we can send them some of our peace by sending them prayers (and food and clothing and shelter) to help them find that quiet place in their hearts and in their homes.

IDEAS...IDEAS...IDEAS

Song:

"Peace Like a River" (see Appendix, page 93)

Lap Sit

Part of working for peace is working together as a community. What better way to illustrate this than by supporting each other, literally!

Ask everyone to stand in a circle close to each other facing into the centre. Everyone then turns a quarter turn in the same direction so they are all facing their neighbour's back. Everyone then puts their hands on the neighbour's waist. The leader says "sit" and everyone sits, making sure their knees are together. It can be hard to keep people from popping out of the circle so you have to work together!

Hearing the Quiet

It is so important to find a way to create time for quiet and silence, time to listen to God and ourselves. Let the members of the group find a comfortable place to sit or lie down. Tell them to close their eyes and take four deep breaths. Ask them to listen to the sounds around them, listen to the quiet, listen for their breathing. After two or three minutes have the children write down all the things they heard.

Peace Tree/Web

Find a large, fallen tree branch or, if there are not any branches available, make a large web using wool or twine on a wood frame, a wire-hanger frame or hula hoop. Have each child make a symbol of peace out of collected materials: shells, stones, leaves, flowers, paper, ribbon, pictures, writing, or whatever else you have on hand. You could also write prayers on the symbols. Hang decorations from the tree or web and put it in the chapel or recreation hall as an offering of a prayer for peace.

Prayer

God, we want to find the peace of day—
the peace of warm sunshine and soft grey clouds,
of gentle rain and the eye of the storm,
peace of the rainbow
the peace of laughter,
and song and silence.
We want to find the peace of the night—
of clear starry skies, cool breezes,
crickets and fireflies,
the peace of safe sleeping
warm toes and good dreams.
Peace be within us—
Peace be with our families.
Peace be with our friends
and with all life on earth.
Amen.

Diversity

Readings

Group life is hard. God actually expects a whole bunch of people with different talents and tastes to get along. God expects that each of us will contribute our skills and together we'll make a community.

When the day of Pentecost had come, they were all together in one place. And suddenly from heaven there came a sound like the rush of a violent wind, and it filled the entire house where they were sitting. Divided tongues, as of fire, appeared among them, and a tongue rested on each of them. All of them were filled with the Holy Spirit and began to speak in different languages, as the Spirit gave them ability.

Adapted from Acts 2:1–4

Now there are all kinds of gifts, but only one Spirit; and there are all kinds of ways to serve, but one God; and there are all kinds of activities, but it is the same God who works through all of them in everyone. To every person is given the power of the Spirit for the common good. To one, wisdom is given through the Spirit; to another, knowledge; to another, faith, by the same Spirit; to another, gifts of healing; to another, the working of miracles; to another, prophecy; to another, the understanding of spiritual matters; to another, various kinds of languages. All these come from one and the same Spirit, who gives each individual their talents just as the Spirit chooses.

Adapted from 1 Corinthians 12:4–11

Hmmms and What Ifs?

According to these readings, not just some people have gifts, skills, and talents but each and every one of us is gifted by the Spirit. Do you know what some of your gifts are? Try to think of five gifts right now. Think of them as presents from God. There is a t-shirt slogan somewhere that says, "God doesn't make junk!" And that's the truth. God created us to be such amazingly wonderful beings that it's only right that we see that in ourselves and thank God for the gifts within us and the gifts of all those around us. But that doesn't always happen. Why do we value some kinds of gifts more than others? How can we make it easier for people to share their gifts? What stops some people from seeing their gifts and talents?

Ideas...Ideas...Ideas

Song:

"Bring Many Names" (see Appendix, page 82)

Nature Scavenger Hunt

This hunt includes only a few categories of items, and the point is to find many variations of the same item. The categories could be: leaves, feathers, soft things, hard things, things that do not change with the seasons, bark/sticks (fallen only). Limit it to five or six general categories. In order that this not become competitive, the group as a whole could have the goal of finding as many different shapes, colours, sizes, and so on, of the items as they can. You will have to set the limits as to what is okay to pick up and what needs to be left in its environment. Then wait to see the wonderful diversity of nature that comes back!

Collage

This is a good follow-up to the nature hunt or a it can be a rainy day activity. Using old magazines or drawings, have children work together to make a collage that illustrates the diversity of nature and of themselves. They can paste on the leaves, twigs, and pictures from their hunt (or from the craft hut) and create either a poster for their group or a banner for chapel.

Heavenly orchestra

There are many ways to make a joyful noise. Here are just a few of them.

Rattles

Materials
- 2 empty cans and lids (removed)
- paper clips, rice, corn, or pebbles
- masking tape or duct tape
- paint or paper

Directions
Put some clips, corn, or whatever you are using into each can. Put lids on top and seal with the tape. Decorate with paint or paper. Shake! Shake! Shake!

Tambourines

Materials
- plastic bottle/jug/lid
- nail or hole punch
- hammer or stone
- pop bottle caps
- wool or string
- scissors

Directions
Cut a 5 cm (2-inch)-wide ring from around the bottle. Poke 10 to 15 holes around the circle. Use a hammer or stone to flatten out the bottle caps. Use a nail to poke a hole through the bottle cap. Feed wool or string through each hole and attach each cap separately to the plastic ring.

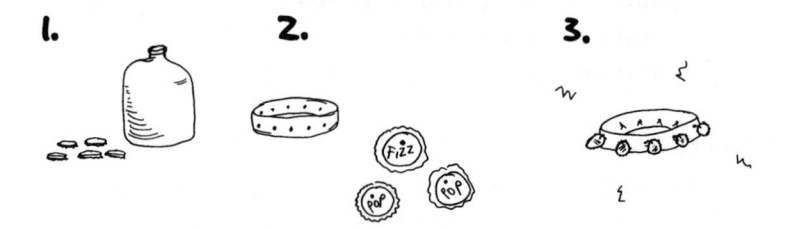

1. **2.** **3.**

Pan Whistle

Materials
- old garden hose or tubing
- small amount of clay
- tape

Directions
Cut the hose or tubing into three sections: 10 cm, 7 cm, and 5 cm (4 inches, 3 inches, and 2 inches) long. Plug up one end of each tube with clay. Put the tubes side by side,

with all open ends lined up evenly and pointing in the same direction, and tape them together across the middle. Blow across the open ends of the tube to make your music!

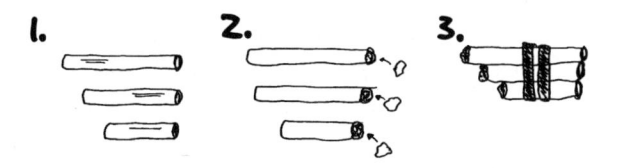

Crossing the Line

This exercise is only suitable for older campers, leaders-in-training or as a staff development exercise. It assumes a level of trust and familiarity among participants. Do not use this as a getting-to-know-you activity.

Have participants stand at one end of a room or area and divide the room in half with a rope or chalk line. The leader will read out a statement and the participants will cross over the line if the statement is true for them. If it is not true, they will stay where they are. You will need to choose or develop statements appropriate to the group you are working with but here are some some sample statements:

- You have felt isolated or rejected because of your race.
- You have stopped someone from making derogatory remarks about someone of a different faith, race, sexual orientation, or economic status.
- You or your family have employed someone of a different race as domestic help.
- You have friends of a different faith.
- You have friends of a different economic class.
- You have been made fun of because of your appearance.

This exercise can be quite a powerful illustration about the ways that we are the same and the ways that we are different and the assumptions we make about people. Ensure that there is some time provided after the exercise to talk with participants about what their experience was and how they felt when they crossed and when they didn't.

Prayer

God of bedbug, ladybug, and every other kind of bug; God of caterpillar and butterfly, hummingbird, and every bird; God of flowers painted red, pink, orange, yellow, and blue, flowers that smell great and those that don't; and for every colour of the rainbow, we thank you. God, we know that you created each one of us in different shapes, sizes, and colours. Help us to respect each person here and to celebrate the ways that we are the same and the ways that we are different. Some of us can draw and dance. Some of us can jump high and others can crawl down low. We each have our own laugh and thoughts and ways of just being ourselves. God, you love (name each child/youth) just the way they are. And we know that you are with us today and always. Amen.

Co-operation

Readings

God's dream for us is community. It takes hard work to get along. It takes hard work to trust each other. It takes hard work to honour each other and what each has to offer. Let's read some mail addressed to folks in the town of Corinth that says something about cooperation.

As it is, there are many parts, yet one body. The eye cannot say to the hand, "I don't need you," nor again the head to the feet, "I don't need you." On the contrary, the parts of the body that seem to be weaker are indispensable, and those members of the body that we think less honourable we clothe with greater honour and greater respect.

                        Adapted from 1 Corinthians 12:20–23

Hmmms and What Ifs?

What are examples in our lives where we need to co-operate with other people to get something done? How can we better work together? What gets in the way of co-operation? What would happen if every counsellor at camp decided to have his or her own camp? Each would have to be the director, the chaplain, and the cook all at once. Imagine the chaos!

Ideas…Ideas…Ideas

Song:
"One Light, One Sun" (see Appendix, page 89)

Rise Up

Divide the children into groups of four, sitting on the ground. They should hang onto the hands or arms of the person next to them and then try to stand up as a unit. If that works, try it with six people or eight—the more people, the harder it becomes.

Knots

Have 8 to 12 people stand in a circle, shoulder to shoulder, and place their hands in the centre. To form the knot everybody needs to grab a couple of hands. You need to make sure that no one holds both hands with the same person or holds the hands of the next person. Now try to untie the knot. You can stip over, duck under, twist and shout, but you can't let go of the hands you're holding. You can also have people outside the knot provide advice on the next move to help untangle the knot.

Islands

Spread hula hoops around the area. While you (or a designated leader) sing a silly song (or play music if a machine is available) the players run around and, when the music stops, the players run to a hoop and step inside. What makes this different from musical chairs is that more than one player can run into each hoop, and the players try to help keep each other in a hoop, which gets more and more difficult as the hoops are slowly removed. It is a real test of group bonding when there is only one hoop left for everyone to fit into!

Progressive Mural

Roll up a long piece of poster paper leaving 15 to 20 cm (6 to 8 inches) unrolled. Pick a theme and have the first person draw, paint, or paste on something that symbolizes that theme. Then unroll another length of the poster paper and ask a second person to add a picture. Continue until the last person has added an image. This mural will be a creation of each and every person in the group. Each group could make a mural and hang them up to decorate the dining hall for a session.

Random Kindness

Perhaps you have seen the bumper sticker "Practise random kindness and senseless acts of beauty." What this refers to is a small but mighty group of people who are secretly out there helping others just because they want to. They don't want medals or awards. They want to practise kindness because it feels good to do so.

What better place to put this into practice than at camp! Maybe it means the next time your neighbour has to clear the table, you get up and do it instead, no questions asked. Maybe it means writing complimentary notes for people in your group or other people at camp and leaving them mysteriously on their bunks for them to find. Maybe it means making a craft for someone who you know is a bit sad and needs cheering up. The possibilities are wonderfully endless!

Prayer

Hand to hand we climb and build your world, O God. Sometimes it might be easier to be alone—when we hurt or when we are angry or upset. But you created us to be a community together, connected as roots to a tree, we grow and are rocked by your wind and rain, and fed by your sun. Help us to help each other to listen and to learn from all your people and to play together to create the world you wish for us. Amen.

Goodbyes

READINGS

"Nothing lasts forever" is a common saying. But the Christian tradition suggests that everything good lasts forever, although not always in the same way. When we are together or apart our memories of our time together hold us close in a different way. Even Jesus felt this way. This is how he said goodbye.

Now before the Passover festival, Jesus, who loved his friends but knew he was going to have to leave them, rose from supper, took off his robe, and tied a towel around himself. He poured water into a bowl and began to wash his friends' feet and to wipe them with the towel. When he was finished he put on his robe, returned to the table, and said to them, "Do you know what I have done for you? I gave you an example that you should do as I have done for you."

Adapted from John 13:1a, 3–5, 12, 15

And Jesus said to them, "Remember, I am with you always, to the end of the age."

Adapted from Matthew 28:20b

HMMMS AND WHAT IFS?

Goodbyes come in lots of different packages. It's one thing to all be saying goodbye at the same time at the end of a session. But it can also be hard when someone has to leave early because of illness or an emergency at home. It is okay to have lots of feelings about saying goodbyes.

Jesus didn't particularly want to leave his friends and family but he knew he had to go. Have there been times when you have had to say goodbye or leave a place when you didn't want to go? How did that feel? How does it feel to be leaving camp? How can we say goodbye to each other?

Jesus also said that even though he was leaving, he would be with them always. What did he mean? How can we take the best things about camp, the spirit of community, the trust, and the fun, back home with us?

IDEAS...IDEAS...IDEAS

Song:

"It Only Takes a Spark" (see Appendix, page 80)

Wizards

All players form a circle and close their eyes. The leader chooses the wizards by tagging their arms. There should be one wizard for every five players. Have everyone open their eyes and run to escape the wizards. At first no one will know who the wizards are except the wizards themselves. Wizards freeze people by tagging them. Players are thawed by being hugged by or shaking hands enthusiastically with another player. Wizards choose new wizards after a few minutes by getting all non-wizards to close their eyes. Wizards choose new wizards by gently touching them on the top of the head.

Souvenirs

Hand-Print T-shirts or Posters

Making designer t-shirts can be lots of fun if you have access to fabric paint or markers and t-shirts. Hand-print posters are fine too if you have access to poster paint and heavy paper. Each child can make a hand print on each other's shirt or poster. Have them sign their names to the hand prints with marker or pen. What a handy souvenir!

Affirmation Sheets

Everyone writes their own name on the top of a piece of paper. Then pass each paper to the right. Write something you have valued, liked, are going to miss about the person whose name is at the top. Keep passing each paper around the circle until everyone has a chance to write on everyone else's sheet.

Prayer

Friend, comforter God, you are always with us. And when it is time to find new beginnings, you love us through the endings. It is hard to say goodbye—goodbye to friends and the warmth of the campfire, goodbye to laughing until you burst and singing until you're hoarse, goodbye to mosquitoes and goodbye to fish sticks [or any other delight particular to your camp].

As we go back to the friends and family that we came from, help us to take our laughter, silliness, friendships, and fun into all that we do. We pray not to forget our time together and our time with you. Amen.

Part Two: Chapel and Vespers

Camp offers a unique and wonderful opportunity to create a community of the moment—to come together for a brief time and, in that time, experience the wonder, the peace, and the love of God. It is a world removed from the ordinary and so offers a different vision of what the church is and can be.

An important part of many church camps are the times of worship throughout the week, at vespers and at chapel. For some children it is their first taste of a "church" that welcomes and affirms their gifts and where laughter and fun are woven with faith stories to create an experience that is not just tolerable but enjoyable.

Pulling together a chapel service or planning for vespers every night can be an intimidating task until you realize that your very best resources are the children and staff who are around you. Find out what their favourite songs are, and include any budding actors in the crowd. If there are children who love to sing, write, or dance, include them. If there are staff who would be willing (on a per session basis) to be part of a planning team, include them. Most people are willing to help if they are asked, and most children will take part in some way if they feel that their contributions will be valued. Not everyone has to be involved in the planning but the more people, the more energy—and the more energy, the more fun.

If nothing else, pray that the children (and the staff) take away with them an experience of God. That doesn't mean it has to be fancy and it doesn't have to be boring, it just needs to come from the heart, to be offered with care and authenticity. And remember that God enjoys a good laugh and a hearty roar and likes people that look silly or people that need to be sad or quiet. It's all okay with God.

Chapel

In many Christian camps chapel is the camp name for church and, like most church services, it usually occurs once a week, generally on Sunday. It can take place indoors or outdoors depending on the weather and facilities.

Chapel is a wonderful opportunity to bring together children's experiences of church and camp, to see the sacred and the holy that surrounds them. And, just like for church services, chapel services do require some advance planning!

Planning and Preparation

Pick a theme and have this be your focus in music and storytelling. There are a number of themes that work well in worship, and some of them are included in this book. Some others are love, joy, respect, and forgiveness.

- Have lots of music planned! For a 30-minute chapel service, there should be at least 3 or 4 songs.
- If you are reading biblical passages, find a translation of the Bible that is written in everyday English.
- Get at least two units or small groups involved with either leading a song, performing a simple skit, developing a group prayer, preparing a banner, or acting or miming your theme topic.
- Choose an overall leader (camper or staff) for the chapel service.
- Keep chapel short, no longer than 30 minutes. Time the service beforehand according to what you have planned. Keep an eye on your watch during chapel and be prepared to go longer if you have more planned and the mood is right.
- It is always better to end on a positive note, so if the

campers are losing interest, build in a song with actions or sing a song in rounds, then finish up as soon as you can.

Be yourself! Lead chapel in ways that are comfortable to you. And encourage your co-leaders to do something challenging but in ways that feel comfortable to them. This sometimes means having a great idea go down the drain if no one can lead the activity, but that's okay.

Suggested Format

This is just one way to organize a chapel service. Use your imagination and knowledge of your group to cut and paste the format to fit.

Welcome

The leader welcomes and quiets the group. Introduce the theme (use a simple sign with large letters). Talk about expected behaviour— listening when people are speaking and readings, and so on.

Opening

Begin with music. Music is a great way to set the mood and bring people into the theme and the "feel" you want to achieve.

Next, read a poem, short paragraph, or story from your own experience to illustrate the theme. Are there biblical readings in which the theme is reflected that could be read or acted out?

Theme Story

Keep the story simple. If your topic is simple, then all you need is an uncomplicated but interesting way to convey it. This can be accomplished in a number of ways:
- Write a short skit that can be read (it doesn't have to be memorized).

- Perform a charade in which the characters have people guess what the theme is.
- Read a very short story—never longer than two minutes (be sure to time yourself first).
- Act a simple role-play revolving around life at camp in which the theme is highlighted.

Activity

Choose something that will allow groups to stay in their places, but lets them express the theme. It is important to have an activity that is reasonably quiet. A yarn circle created from individual pieces of yarn works well with the themes of co-operation or diversity. A candle passed around could illustrate the theme of peace.

Change Up

(changing the mood)
Choose a song that is lively. Perhaps there is someone at camp who can help out by playing a guitar or other instrument.

Closing

Conclude with a story or spoken word about your theme that reflects hope for tomorrow and the ways that the theme symbolizes this particular community. Use examples from camp and how the theme can make a difference at camp and in campers' lives. Sometimes humorous examples can make a point as well as serious ones.

Finish with music— either quietly powerful or rousing, depending on the mood you want to achieve.

Vespers

Vespers, or evening prayer, is usually a simple, quiet and beautiful way to end the night. It is less boisterous than campfire and often is time for music, prayer, and storytelling. Some people find it comforting to use the same format for vespers each night and change only the content of the prayers or story. Others create new services each night. Either way, vespers is usually a much shorter service, no longer than 15 minutes or so. Although vespers certainly can be held indoors, most camps prefer the great outdoors, in the forest, by the water, or around a fire.

Planning and Preparation

Vespers can pick up on the theme for the day or week through prayers and music, or can be planned with the same basic format and theme for the entire session or summer. It is a good idea to know which format you want to use before the beginning of a session so that it will be consistent each night.

Like chapel, it is good to have a designated leader for vespers. One of the benefits of having a simple structure is that is usually easy to get campers involved in the leadership.

In choosing music for vespers try to think of songs that can be sung while going to and returning from the site of vespers, songs that are quiet, and songs that seem to close the day.

Suggested format
Getting There

Making your way to the location where vespers are held can be the beginning of the service. You can sing or chant quietly as you walk.

Gathering

Arrive singing or begin with a song that can be sung over and over until everyone arrives and forms a circle.

Prayer

Offer a simple prayer to bring people together to give God thanks for the day and give an opportunity for campers and staff to say what has been meaningful to them that day. A time of silence is also good as people gather their thoughts and offer silent prayers.

Story

This is a time when the storytellers in your group can really help out. Often, because it is night and usually campers are slightly less energetic, they are more inclined to listen to a story. It is better to tell the story than to read it but reading is okay too, just speak slowly, loudly, and clearly.

Closing song

Just what it sounds like ... a quiet song to send people to their sleeping bags and to close the day.

Part Three:
Food for Thought:
Giving Thanks

Here are some oldies and some new songs and prayers to give thanks for our daily bread ... and pasta ... and lettuce ... and jello....

For Health and Strength

(F chord throughout)

For health and strength and dai-ly food, we give you thanks, O God.

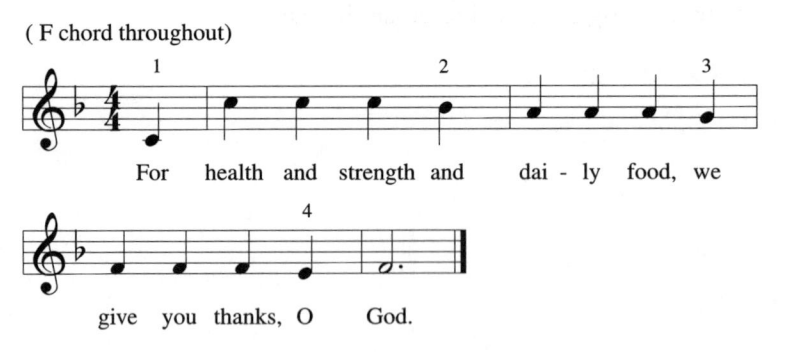

Can be sung as a round.

64 *Gathered 'Round*

Johnny Appleseed

(F chord throughout)

Ohhh... The Lord is good to me and
so I thank the Lord for giv - ing me the
things I need, the sun and the rain and the
ap - ple - seed. The Lord is good to me!

Ohhh... For ev - 'ry seed I sow an
ap - ple - seed will grow and some - day there'll be
ap - ples there for ev - 'ry - one in the
world to share. The Lord is good to me!

Last time only

John - ny Ap - ple - seed. A - men!

Hot Meal Grace

Thank you, God for the rain and land.
Thank you, God for our work-ing hands.
Thank you for food for bod-y and soul, and
if we keep thank-ing it's gon-na get cold! It's
gon-na get col-der and we're gon-na get older, so we'd bet-ter get bold-er and eat!

Words and music: Linnea Good
Copyright © 1989 Borealis Music.

66 *Gathered 'Round*

Banquet Earth Grace

Cha - pa - thi, Cha - pa - thi, Pu - ri and rice! Bur-ri - to, ta - qui - to, spa - ghet - ti and spice! Dim sum, egg foo yong, Two all- beef pat - ties, spec - ial sauce on a bun. Hands a - cross the ta - ble, hands a - cross the sea, Shar - ing in the ban - quet of the earth! Thanks!

Notes are given to show rhythm. Typically this grace is chanted or shouted.

Words and music: Linnea Good
Copyright © 1989 Borealis Music.

Praise God for Bread

Morn - ing
Noon - time has come, the board is spread.
Eve - ning

Thanks be to God who gives us bread;

praise God for bread!

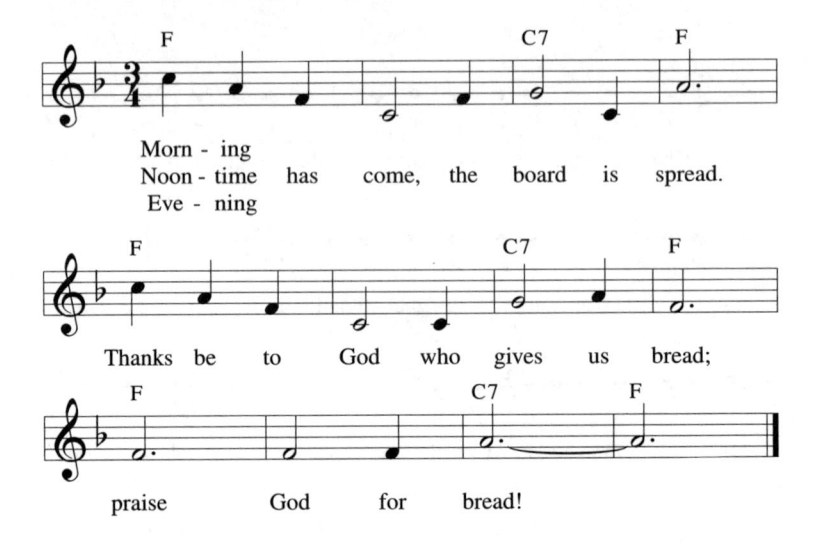

Choose the opening word to suit the time of day.

Attributed to A.R. Ledoux

Hark to the Chimes

Hark to the chimes, come bow your head.

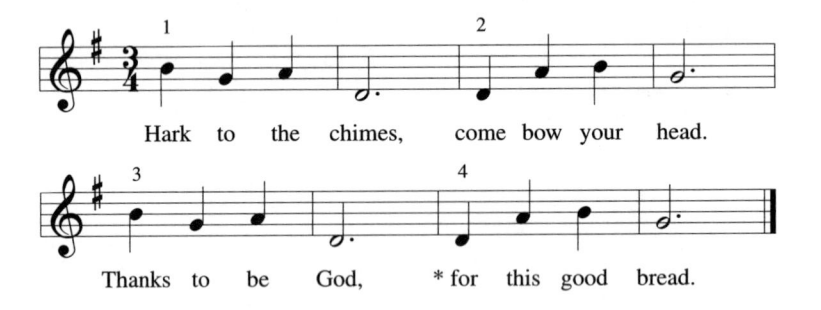

Thanks to be God, * for this good bread.

Can be sung as a round. (*) may be sung "who gives us bread."

68 *Gathered 'Round*

Thank You God

(to the tune of "Glory Glory Hallelujah")

Thank you God for fish sticks,
    (or spaghetti or whatever the selection is)
Thank you God for fish sticks,
Thank you God for fish sticks,
We give you thanks.

God is Great

(to the tune of "Rock around the Clock")

God is great. God is good.
And we thank God for our food.
We're gonna thank God
morning, noon and night
our God, our God, is outta sight
amen, amen, amen, amen, amen
cha cha cha.

Part Four: Home Away from Home

The following ideas are intended to help both staff and campers feel good about being at camp and to welcome them and show them that they have an important place in the community.

Covenanting Service for Camp Staff

The beginning of a summer in the life of a camp can be absolutely crazy. Are there enough supplies? Are the cabins ready? Who are the new staff? What will the campers be like? Will I survive?

Amid the early chaos of staff orientation, hold a covenanting service and invite all staff—including maintenance and kitchen staff—to attend. The intent of this service is to begin to build bridges of support and understanding with each other and to see the work of all as vitally important to the camp. Because many camps include staff from a variety of religious and non-religious backgrounds, and because the goal is inclusivity, I have tried to make the language as inclusive as possible. Please take this as only one way to covenant with each other and modify the service to reflect the needs of your community.

OPENING WORDS

These are opening remarks from the Director or chaplain or designated leader, welcoming all to camp and to this time together.

CALL TO WORSHIP

(The leader holds a candle—each staff member also has a small candle).

Let us remember who we are (leader lights the candle).

Leader: This camp has been here for (number of years) years. Over that time many people have felt called to give of their time, their talents, and their love, and to gather underneath the stars and sun and make this camp their home.

People: **We light a candle for all those who have touched the lives of children, parents, and colleagues—a light of compassion and gentleness.**

Leader: We are called not only to act, but to be—to be faithful to ourselves and to each other, to risk enough to show the power of love, and to make a place of laughter and acceptance in the world.

People: **We light a candle for our hopes and dreams, that they might be glimpsed among the trees and in the wind and that our time here will build in us a place of peace and strength.**

Leader: All of us come with our own expectations and experiences. What are some of your hopes and dreams for the summer?

(Invite staff to say a few words if they want to.)

Leader: All of us are about to enter into a covenant relationship. This means that we are making promises to each other and also that we are held in our promise by the Creator's love. All of you have a reason for being here and it is more than a summer job—being at camp requires a spirit of giving and a respect for creation and for each other. Do you as staff promise to support each other and to

> grow together, to laugh together and to build a community that welcomes children (youth/families) and treats them with respect and care?

People: **We do.**

Leader: As a sign of this promise, please come and light your candle.

(As each staff comes forward and lights a candle, the leader greets each by name and says "welcome." When all candles are lit and everyone is back in place in the circle, the leader continues.)

Leader: These flames are to give light to your path and serve as a reminder of the promises we have made to each other. Let us sing together.

SENDING YOU LIGHT

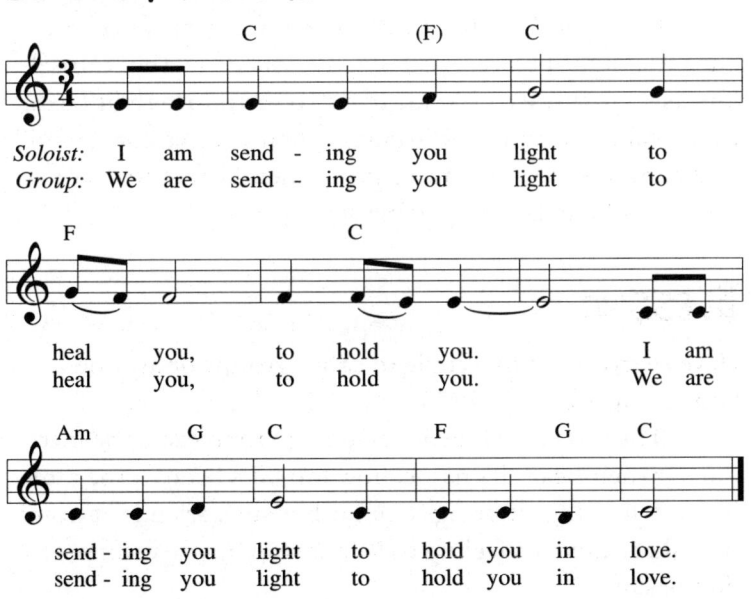

Soloist: I am send-ing you light to heal you, to hold you. I am send-ing you light to hold you in love.

Group: We are send-ing you light to heal you, to hold you. We are send-ing you light to hold you in love.

Words and music: Melanie DeMore

Leader: Amen. Let's have a great summer.

Part Four: *Home Away from Home*

Blessing of the Bears

This blessing is for bears (of the stuffed variety) or bunnies or blankets or any other friends that campers and leaders may have brought with them to feel secure. It would be good to use this at the beginning of camp, especially if some of your campers or staff are homesick. It could be a part of a vespers service or used in cabin groups after vespers.

Preparation

It might be good to announce the service in advance, perhaps the night before. It can be introduced by the counsellors as something they want to do to introduce their bears to the cabin or camp and to make them feel welcome, and that campers are welcome to bring their bears too. If it's not too cold, make it a pajama service.

Blessing

Have everyone sit in a circle in cabin groups or around a large campfire.

The director and counsellors go first, each one introducing their bear—its name, how long it's been in the family, and greetings it brings from other such friends at home. And share how it's feeling to be at camp. Invite campers to do the same.

After everyone has introduced their bear, talk about what it's like to come to camp and to sleep away from home, and assure the bears that they are welcome at camp and that they have a very important job of taking care of the cabins during the day while the campers have all the fun.

Prayer
Thank you God for bears, and bunnies, and other squishy, soft, fuzzy friends that give great hugs. They help us feel safe and loved here at camp and they are great at keeping secrets. We know that you also take care of us when we sleep and all through the day—loving us, protecting us, and opening up your world for us to see. Amen.

The leader goes around to each camper with stickers (heart, star, happy face, etc.), one for the camper and one for the bear, and says, "welcome."

After all campers, staff, bears, and bunnies have been stickered, pass around a big bowl of popcorn to seal the deal.

Cabin Prayers

These are some suggestions if the campers want to say prayers before bed.

A child's night prayer
*God of the stars
God of the moon,
God on the earth
God in my room.
Be in my teddy,
Be in my head,
Be in my dreams
floating over my bed.
God of the morning,
God of the night,
Hold me and keep me
'Til dawn's early light.*

From *Out of the fire: Worship and Theology of Liberation*, Gertrude Lebans. Published by artemis enterprises. Copyright © 1992. Used by permission.

Now I lay me down to sleep
*Now I lay me down to sleep
the moon, the stars, my friends to keep
and with your wind and gentle rain
wake me in your love again.
Amen.*

We thank you God
*We thank you God for the moon and sun
for games and songs and summer fun
Thanks for the day.
Amen.*

Bless us in our sleeping bags
Bless us in our sleeping bags
Bless us in our jammies
Protect us in the dark of night
and keep us from all whammies!
Good night!

Appendix Music

Music is one of the most wonderful ways we connect with each other and with God. What is included here is just a smackeral of the bounty of great songs to be sung at camp. I hope that you will see some favorites and some new ones too. Sing out, sing out, wherever you are!

Go Now in Peace

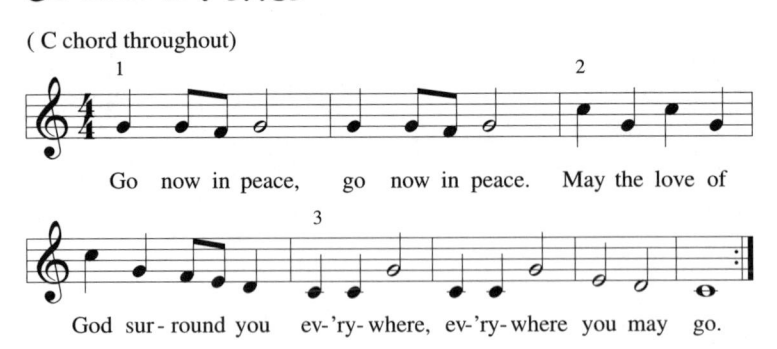

(C chord throughout)

Go now in peace, go now in peace. May the love of God sur-round you ev-'ry-where, ev-'ry-where you may go.

Can be sung as a round.

Words and music: Natalie Sleeth
Copyright © 1976 by Hinshaw Music, Inc. Used with permission

The Garden Song

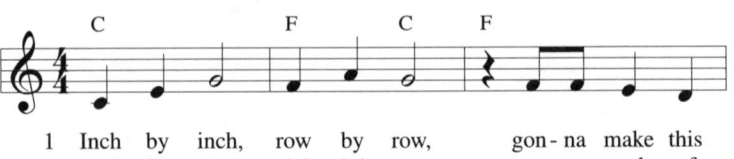

1 Inch by inch, row by row, gon-na make this
2 Pull-in' weeds, pick-in' stones, we are made of
3 Make your rows straight and long, tem-per them with

gar - den grow, all it takes is a rake and a hoe and a
dreams and bones, I feel a need to grow my own for the
warmth and song, moth- er earth will make you strong if you

piece of fer - tile ground. Inch by inch,
time is near at hand. Grain for grain,
give her love and care. See that crow watching

row by row some- one bless these seeds I sow,
sun and rain, find my way thru' na - ture's chain
hun - gri - ly from his perch on yon - der tree,

— some- one warm them from be - low till the
as I tune my bod - y and my brain to the
— in my gar - den I'm as free as that

rain comes tum - bl - ing down.
mu - sic of the land.
fea - thered thief up there.

Words and music: David Mallet
Copyright © 1975 Cherry Lane Music Publishing Company, Inc. (ASCAP)/DreamWorks Songs (ASCAP). Worldwide rights for DreamWorks Songs administered by Cherry Lane Music Publishing Company, Inc. International Copyright Secured. All Rights Reserved. Used by permission of Cherry Lane Music Company.

It Only Takes a Spark

1. It only takes a spark to get a fire going, and soon all those around can warm up in its glowing: that's how it is with God's love, once you've experienced it: you spread God's love to everyone, you want to pass it on.

2. What a wondrous time is spring when all the trees are budding, the birds begin to sing, the flowers start their blooming; that's how it is with God's love, once you've experienced it: you want to sing, it's fresh like spring, you want to pass it on.

3. I wish for you, my friend, this happiness that I've found — on God you can depend, it matters not where you're bound; I'll shout it from the mountain top; I want my world to know: the Lord of love has come to me, I want to pass it on.

Words and music: Kurt Kaiser 1969
Words and music used by permission of Budjohn Songs.

THE SPIRIT IN ME

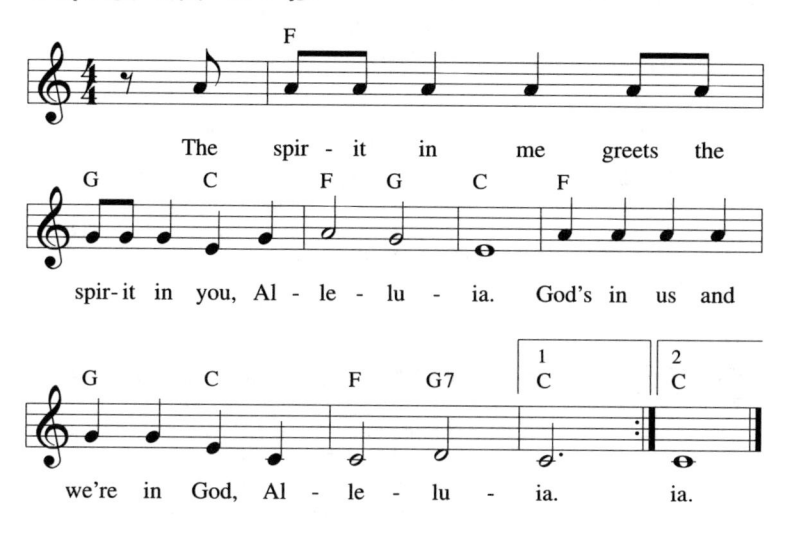

(musical notation with lyrics:)

The spir-it in me greets the spir-it in you, Al-le-lu-ia. God's in us and we're in God, Al-le-lu-ia. ia.

Repeat as often as needed, as a greeting for a gathering or as a closing, with a variety of appropriate actions. This song has been used with a type of "laying on of hands" ceremony. Some people use the gesture of respect of the people of India — hands together (as if in prayer) in front of the chest. Others use these actions:

The spirit in me	*(point to self)*
Greets the spirit in you	*(point to someone else)*
Alleluia	*(hands open and raised)*
God's in us	*(grab hands)*
And we're in God	*(cross hands over chest)*
Alleluia	*(open hands, arms spread)*

Words and music: Jim Strathdee
Copyright © 1972 by Desert Flower Music, P.O. Box 1476, Carmichael, CA 95609. Used by Permission.

Bring Many Names

1. Bring man-y names, beau-ti-ful and good, cel-e-brate, in par-a-ble and story, ho-li-ness in glo-ry, liv-ing, lov-ing God. Hail and ho-
2. Strong mo-ther God, work-ing night and day, plan-ning all the won-ders of cre-a-tion, set-ting each e-qua-tion, gen-i-us at play: Hail and ho-
3. Warm fa-ther God, hug-ging ev-ery child, feel-ing all the strains of hu-man liv-ing, car-ing and for-giv-ing till we're re-con-ciled: Hail and ho-
4. Old, ach-ing God, grey with end-less care, calm-ly pierc-ing e-vil's new dis-guis-es, glad of good sur-pris-es, wis-er than de-spair: Hail and ho-

82 Gathered 'Round

san - na! Bring man - y names!
san - na, strong moth - er God!
san - na, warm fa - ther God!
san - na, old, ach - ing God!

great liv - ing God!

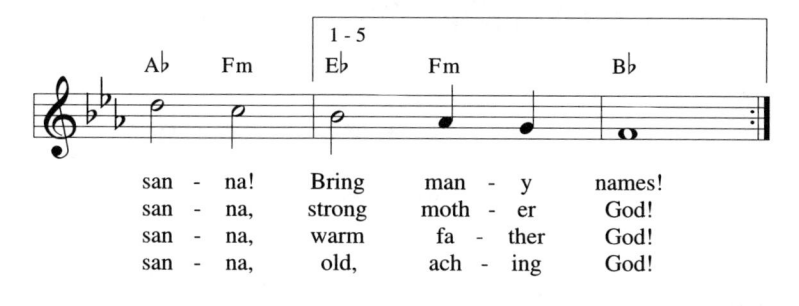

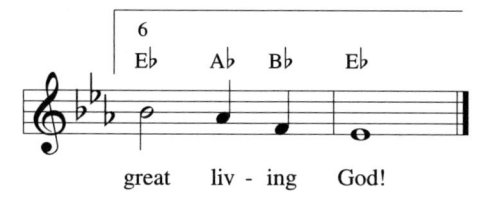

5. Young, growing God,
   eager, on the move,
   saying no to falsehood
      and unkindness,
   crying out for justice,
   giving all you have:
   Hail and hosanna,
   young, growing God!

6. Great living God,
   never fully known,
   joyful darkness far beyond
      our seeing,
   closer yet than breathing,
   everlasting home:
   Hail and hosanna,
   great, living God!

Words: Brian Wren 1986, alt. 1993 ·
Music: Carlton R. Young, 1987
Words and music copyright © 1989 Hope Publishing Company.

Music 83

Lying in My Sleeping Bag

Ly-ing in my sleep-ing bag, I could-n't fall a-sleep I looked at my watch, and I want-ed to weep. I rolled to the left and I rolled to the right and I heard ev-'ry sound that you can hear at night! And this is what I heard,

(1) I heard a cric-ket ch ch ch ch ch ch ch ch ch ch ch

(2) I heard a dog ar ar ar ooo ar ar ar ooo

84 *Gathered 'Round*

(3) I heard a si-ren whee oo whee oo whee oo whee oo

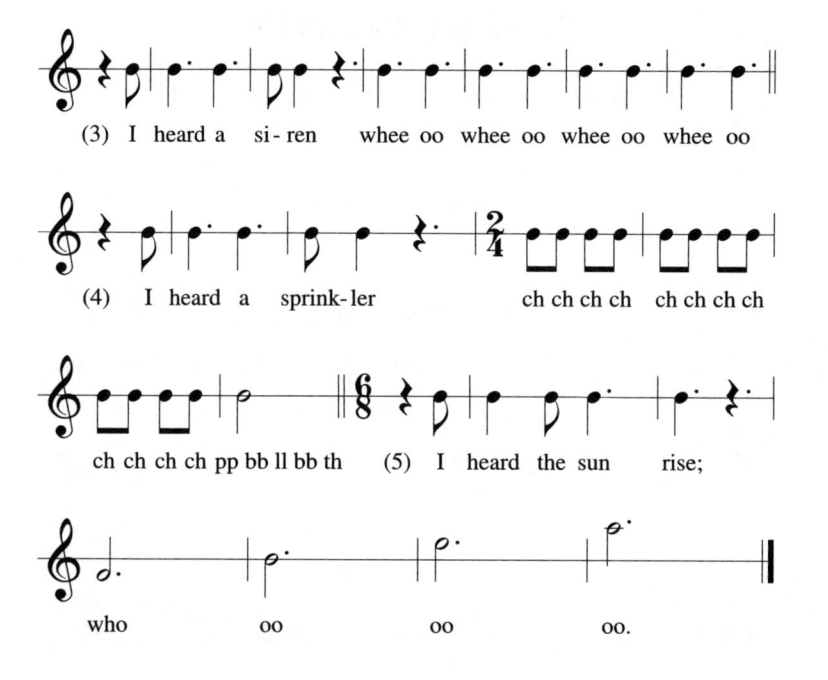

(4) I heard a sprink-ler ch ch ch ch ch ch ch ch

ch ch ch ch pp bb ll bb th (5) I heard the sun rise;

who oo oo oo.

This piece is usually done as a rap song; the notes are given only to convey rhythm. The sound for the sunrise in the last four bars should glide upward, from low to high voice.

Words and music: Linnea Good
Copyright © 1988 Borealis Music.

LET THERE BE PEACE ON EARTH

Let there be peace on earth and let it be-gin with me. Let there be peace on earth, the peace that was meant to be. With God as Cre-a-tor, chil-dren all are we. Let us walk with each o-ther in per-fect har-mo-ny. Let peace be-gin with me, let this be the mo-ment now. With ev-'ry step I take, let this be my sol-emn vow; to take each mo-ment and live each mo-ment in peace e-ter-nal-ly. Let there be peace on earth and let it be-gin with me.

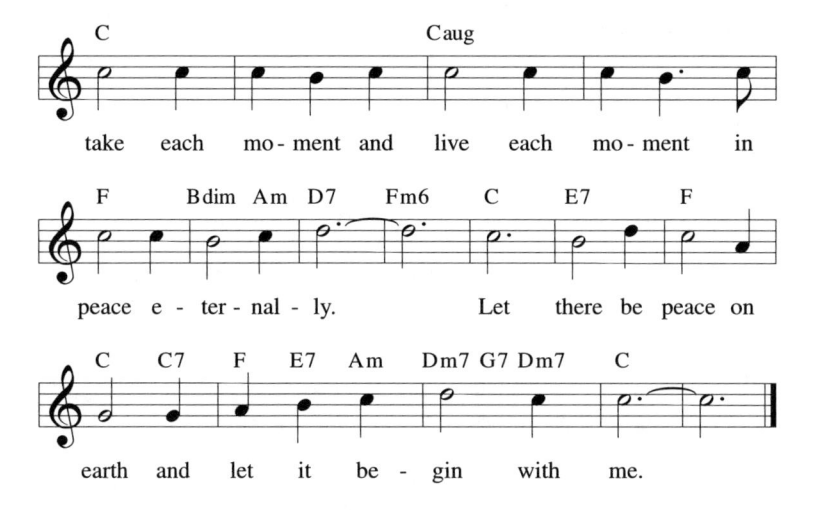

Words and music by Sy Miller and Jill Jackson.
Copyright by Jan-Lee Music 1955; renewed 1983. Used by permission.

FRIENDS

Friends are some-thing when we sing to-geth-er, when we sing the whole day, when we sing the night a-way, when we sing to-geth-er, when we { sing. laugh. pray.

Music 87

Kum Ba Yah

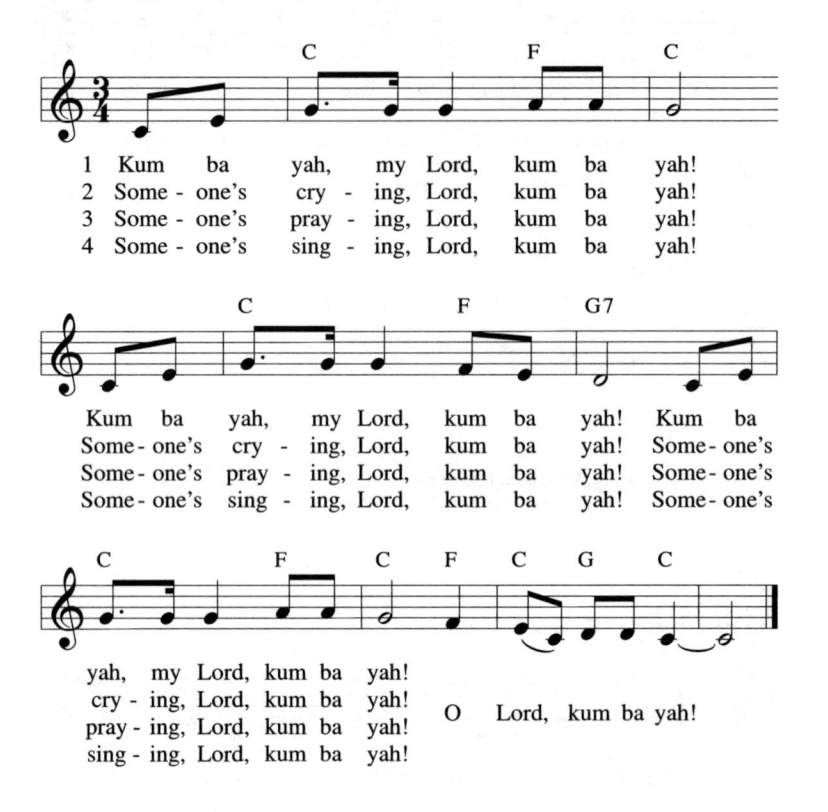

1 Kum ba yah, my Lord, kum ba yah!
2 Some-one's cry-ing, Lord, kum ba yah!
3 Some-one's pray-ing, Lord, kum ba yah!
4 Some-one's sing-ing, Lord, kum ba yah!

Kum ba yah, my Lord, kum ba yah! Kum ba
Some-one's cry-ing, Lord, kum ba yah! Some-one's
Some-one's pray-ing, Lord, kum ba yah! Some-one's
Some-one's sing-ing, Lord, kum ba yah! Some-one's

yah, my Lord, kum ba yah!
cry-ing, Lord, kum ba yah!   O Lord, kum ba yah!
pray-ing, Lord, kum ba yah!
sing-ing, Lord, kum ba yah!

"Kum ba yah" is a pidgin-English rendering of "Come by here." There is almost no limit to the number of possible verses. The progression of "crying... praying... singing..." often moves on to "Someone's laughing, Lord..." and "Someone's happy, Lord..." The first verse is often sung as a chorus or used to conclude the song.

88 *Gathered 'Round*

ONE LIGHT, ONE SUN

1. One light, one sun, one sun lighting ev-'ry-one.
2. One world, one home, one world home for ev-'ry-one.
3. One love, one heart, one heart warming ev-'ry-one.

One world turning, one world turning ev-'ry-one.
One dream, one song, one song heard by ev-'ry-one.
One hope, one joy, one love filling ev-'ry-one.

Coda

One light, one sun, one sun lighting ev-'ry-one. One light warming ev-'ry-one.

Words and music: Raffi
Copyright ©1985 Homeland Publishings (SOCAN), a division of Troubadour Records Ltd.
All rights reserved. Used by permission.

Psalm 100 – Make a Joyful Noise

Refrain

Make a joy-ful noise all the earth!
Wor-ship your God with glad-ness.
Make a joy-ful noise all the earth.
Come to this place with a song! song!

Verses

1. Know that your God has made you. Know it's to God we be-long. And
2. En-ter these gates, thanks giv-ing. En-ter these courts with praise. Sing
3. A-ges through end-less a-ges, sea-sons of end-less years, the

90 *Gathered 'Round*

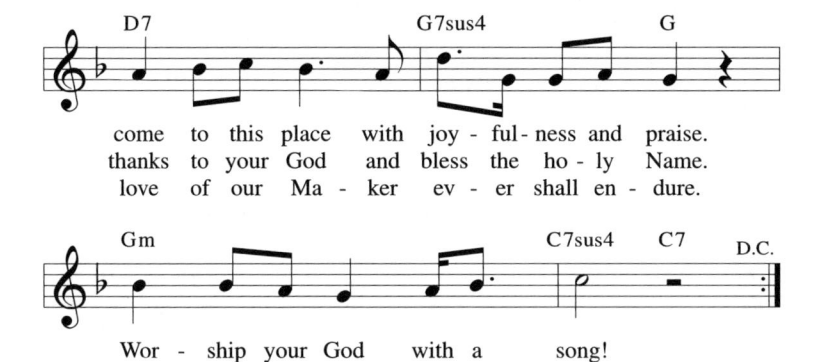

come to this place with joy-ful-ness and praise.
thanks to your God and bless the ho-ly Name.
love of our Ma-ker ev-er shall en-dure.

Wor - ship your God with a song!

Words and music: Linnea Good 1991
Copyright © 1991 Borealis Music.

Day is Done

Day is done, gone the sun, from the lake, from the hills, from the sky. All is well, safe-ly rest, God is nigh.

Music 91

Rise and Shine

Refrain

Rise and shine and give God the glo-ry, glo-ry.
Rise and shine and give God the glo-ry, glo-ry.
Rise and shine and give God the glo-ry, glo-ry:
chil-dren of our God.

1. God said to Noah, "There's gon-na be a floody, floody *(twice)*
   Get those children out of the muddy, muddy," Children of our God.

2. So Noah, he built him, he built him an arky, arky *(twice)*
   Made it out of Gopher barky, barky, Children of our God.

3. The animals, they came in by two-zies, two-zies *(twice)*
   Elephants and kangaroo-zies, roo-zies, Children of our God.

4. It rained and poured for forty day-zies, day-zies *(twice)*
   Nearly drove those animals crazies, craizies, Children of our God.

5. Dove went out, to take a peeky, peeky *(twice)*
   Dove came back with twig in beaky, beaky, Children of our God.

6. The animals came out in three-zies, three-zies, three-zies *(twice)*
   Must have been those birds and bee-zies, bee-zies, Children of our God.

7. This is the end of our story, story *(twice)*
   Everything is hunky-dory, dory, Children of our God.

According to the King James Version of the Bible, God told Noah to build the ark out of gopher-wood (Genesis 6:14 *KJV*).

Peace Like a River

I've got peace like a river, I've got peace like a river, I've got peace like a river in my soul, I've got peace like a river, I've got peace like a river, I've got peace like a river in my soul!

Shabbat Shalom (Welcome Shabbat)

Bim bam bim bim bim bam, bim bim bim bim bim bam.

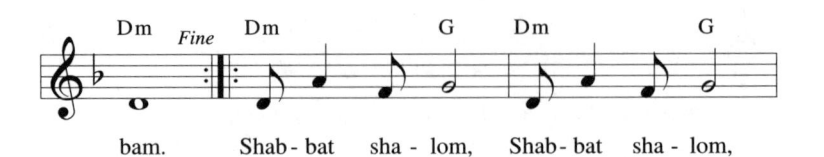

Shab-bat sha-lom, Shab-bat sha-lom,

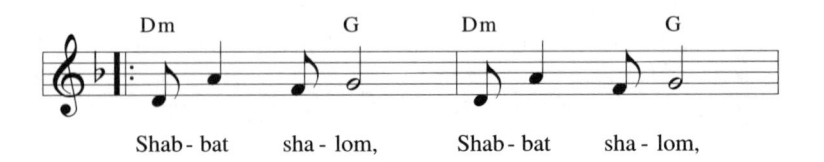

Shab-bat Shab-bat, Shab-bat, Shab-bat sha-lom.

Shab-bat, Shab-bat, Shab-bat, Shab-bat sha-lom.

Shab-bat sha-lom, Shab-bat sha-lom,

Shab-bat, Shab-bat, Shab-bat, Shab-bat sha-lom.

"SHABBAT SHALOM" from Manginot: 201 Songs for Jewish Schools © 1992 Transcontinental Music Publications, 838 Fifth Avenue, New York, NY 10021. Email: tmp@uahc.org

WHAT DOES THE LORD REQUIRE?

What does the Lord require of you?
What does the Lord require of you?
Jus - tice, kind - ness, walk hum - bly with your God.
To seek jus - tice, and love kind - ness, and walk hum - bly with your God.

This can be sung as a regular round, but Jim Strathdee recommends a three-part rendition, with basses on part 1, tenors and altos on part 2, and sopranos on part 3. The voices enter one at a time and repeat their part until it is time to end the song.

Music: Jim Strathdee
Copyright © 1986 by Desert Flower Music, P.O. box 1476, Carmichael, CA 95609. Used by permission.

WE ARE MARCHING

Collected and edited by Anders Nyberg

We are march-ing in the light of God, we are marching in the light of God. We are march-ing in the light of God, we are march-ing in the light of God. We are march-ing, the light of God. We are march-ing, march-ing, we are

Si-ya-hamb' e-ku-kha-nyen' kwen-khos', si-ya-hamb' e-ku-kha-nyen' kwen-khos'. Si-ya-hamb' e-ku-kha-nyen' kwen-khos', si-ya-hamb' e-ku-kha-nyen' kwen-khos'. Si-ya-ham-ba, kha-nyen' kwen-khos'. Si-ya-ham-ba, ham-ba, si-ya-

Copyright © 1984 Utryck. Used by permission of Walton Music Corp.

Music 97

Ha-La-La-La

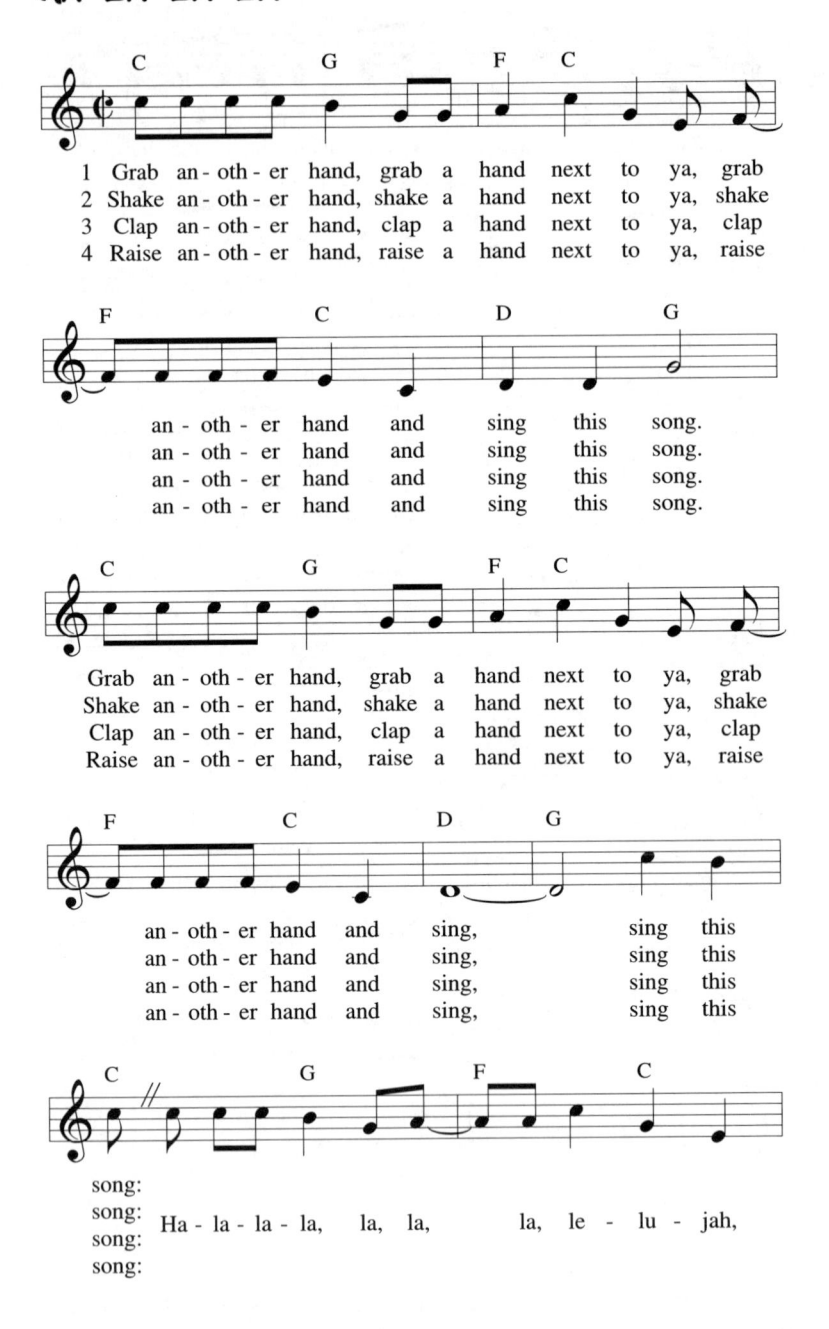

1. Grab an-oth-er hand, grab a hand next to ya, grab an-oth-er hand and sing this song.
2. Shake an-oth-er hand, shake a hand next to ya, shake an-oth-er hand and sing this song.
3. Clap an-oth-er hand, clap a hand next to ya, clap an-oth-er hand and sing this song.
4. Raise an-oth-er hand, raise a hand next to ya, raise an-oth-er hand and sing this song.

Grab an-oth-er hand, grab a hand next to ya, grab an-oth-er hand and sing, sing this song:
Shake an-oth-er hand, shake a hand next to ya, shake an-oth-er hand and sing, sing this song:
Clap an-oth-er hand, clap a hand next to ya, clap an-oth-er hand and sing, sing this song:
Raise an-oth-er hand, raise a hand next to ya, raise an-oth-er hand and sing, sing this song:

Ha-la-la-la, la, la, la, le-lu-jah,

Almost any action within reason can be incorporated into this song: Scratch another back... Pat another head... Hug another friend....

Words and music: David Graham
Copyright © 1978 C. A. Music (div. of C. A. Records, Inc.). All rights reserved. Used by permission.

Spirit of Rock and Tree

1. Spirit of rock and tree, spirit of sky and sea, spirit of me, moon and sun, all are one. Day is done.
2. Spirit of rock and tree, spirit of sky and sea, spirit of me, below low above, snake and dove, held in love.
3. Spirit of rock and tree, spirit of sky and sea, spirit of me, moon and sun, all are one. Day is done. Day is done.

Words and music: Kim McKellar 1997
Copyright © 1997 Kim McKellar.

INDEX OF FIRST LINES AND COMMON TITLES

Banquet Earth Grace 67
Bring many names, beautiful and good 82
Chapathi, chapathi, puri and rice 67
Day is done 91
For health and strength and daily food 64
Friends are something when we sing together 87
The Garden Song 78
Go now in peace 78
God is Great 69
Grab another hand, grab a hand next to ya 98
Ha-La-La-La 98
Hark to the chimes 68
Hot Meal Grace 66
I am sending you light to heal you 73
Inch by inch, row by row 78
It only takes a spark to set a fire going 80
I've got peace like a river 93
Johnny Appleseed 65
Kum by yah, my Lord, kum ba yah! 88
Let there be peace on earth and let it begin with me 86
Lying in my sleeping bag 84
Make a joyful noise all the earth 90
Morning has come, the board is spread 68
Ohhh...The Lord is good to me 65
One light, one sun, one sun lighting ev'ryone 89
Peace Like a River 93
Praise God for Bread 68
Rise and shine and give God the glory, glory 92
Sending You Light 73
Shabbat shalom 94
Siyahamba 96
The spirit in me greets the spirit in you 81
Spirit of rock and tree 100
Thank you God 69
Thank you, God for the rain and land 66
We are marching in the light of God (Siyahamba) 96
What does the Lord require of you? 95

Resource Bibliography

This list of resources contains some of the materials that I have found particularly helpful or that have been recommended to me by other camp folk and youth workers, and is by no means exhaustive. And by the way, when you've finished this book, you are the best resource you can offer a group of young people. Trust your experience and your wisdom and the group you are working with. These resources are a jump start for your own imagination and creativity.

The games, activities, and music gathered for this resource come from a variety of sources. The same activity that is a long-standing tradition at one camp will be brand new for another. Some will seem familiar but then, just when you least expect it, offer a new twist or turn. Activities such as these are meant to be modified, altered, and cut and pasted to suit the people who are gathered. And so, their changes get passed on and then the changes to the changes, and so on, and so on, until it is nearly impossible to identify an "original source." That said, where it has been possible, sources and copyright holders have been acknowledged.

LEADERSHIP

Hopkins, Susan and Jeffrey Winters, eds. *Discover the World: Empowering Children to Value Themselves and Others and the Earth*. Philadelphia: New Society Publishers, 1990. Ideas and stories from teachers and leaders who are working to empower children through new ways of relating to children as part of the Christian community.

Committee on Outdoor Ministry. *Leadership Development Notebook.* Committee on Outdoor Ministry, Education for Christian Life and mission, National Council of Churches, 1983. This was designed as the basic manual for the North American Church Camp. Thirty topics are divided into four training sections: theology and faith development, community and self-understanding, program planning, and camping skills.

Committee on Outdoor Ministry. *Supplement to Leadership Development Notebook.* Committee on Outdoor Ministry, Education for Christian Life and Mission, National Council of Churches, 1988. Contains supplementary leadership training modules that include nine new themes: building self-esteem, suicide awareness, sexual abuse, volunteer and paid staff working together, multicultural education, holistic camping, toward human equality, sharing the faith story, and computer basics.

Tindal, Mardi and Bill McDonald. *Who Me - A Theologian? Models for Theologizing In a Camp or Other Informal Setting.* Toronto: Division of Mission in Canada, The United Church of Canada, 1981.

WORSHIP/MUSIC

All God's Children Sing: The children's music resources. Winfield, B.C.: Wood Lake Books, 1992.

Break, Jean, ed. *Magic Ring.* American Camping Association, 1985. A wonderful collection of poetry for vespers or morning watch.

CGIT (Canadian Girls in Training) Songbook. National CGIT Association. Available from CGIT Association, 195 The West Mall, Suite 414, Etobicoke, ON, M9C 5K1.

Come Join the Circle Songbook. Brethren Press, 1988. Contains 44 songs, specially produced for outdoor ministries.

Farquharson, Walter and Ron Klusmeier. *Just Like Salt: 25 Songs of Faith for Children.* Worship Arts, Ottawa, 1985.

I Will Gladly Sing: A Song Book for Youth Ministry. Episcopal Church Centre, 1984. A wonderful song book that was produced for the 1984 National Episcopal Youth Event. It is available for US$1.00 from the Episcopal Church Centre, 815 - 2nd Ave., New York, NY 10017, USA.

Manley, Jim. *Seed Songs of Earth and Spirit.* 1983. Music written in response to the National Council of Churches Outdoor Ministry theme concerning God's creation, our place in the world and with each other.

Middleton, Kate and Mardi Tindal. *Spirit of Singing.* Winfield, B.C.: Wood Lake Books, 1994. This is an excellent compilation of songs that have been sung around the campfire for years, and songs that are just beginning to be favourites.

Milton, Ralph. *Living God's Way: Bible stories retold for children in today's world.* Winfield, B.C.: Wood Lake Books, 1992. An excellent retelling of biblical stories for children.

White, William. *Speaking in Stories: Resources for Christian Storytellers.* Augsburg Press, 1982.

White, William. *Stories for Telling: A Treasury for Christian Storytellers.* Augsburg Press, 1986.

Wilson, Lois. *Miriam, Mary and Me — Women in the Bible. Stories Retold for Children and Adults.* Winfield, B.C.: Wood Lake Books, 1992.

Program

There are a number of educational resources produced by the United Church's Division of Mission in Canada that are adaptable to camping situations:

Children for Peace, 1991. Six sessions to help children talk about their fears for the world, analyze harmful practices, such as prejudice and war, and grow in confidence by doing something positive to work for peace, justice, and a safe environment.

In Care of Creation, 1989. Four sessions designed to help children explore the interconnectedness of all created things and their place as caretakers in creation.

See Me, See Us, 1992. Five sessions for younger children (five to eight) that focus on friendship and group-building skills.

Who We Are, 1988. Five sessions for younger children (five to eight) to help them explore who they are and their place in caring for the earth and all God's creatures.

OTHER PROGRAM RESOURCES

Drake, Jane and Ann Love. *The Kid's Cottage Book*. Toronto: Kids Can Press Ltd., 1993. Over a hundred environmentally friendly ideas for things to make or do — rainy day games, songs, crafts, and more.

Don't Panic! The Essential Youth Ministry Manual. Hamilton, ON: Diocese of Niagara, Anglican Church of Canada, 1994. A comprehensive how, why, and what manual for ministry with youth. Good material of planning, evaluation, styles of leadership and resources for community building, worship, games and activities, music, and more.

Gooch, John. *Is My Nose Growing?* Nashville: Abingdon Press, 1992. This is a "best of" compilation of 30 sessions that incorporate worship and bible study as part of every program (from the United Methodist *Discoveries in Faith* material).

Hanson, Bob and Bill Roemmich, eds. *Stories for the Campfire*. American Camping Association, 1983.

Marcum, Walt. *Sharing Groups in Youth Ministry*. Nashville: Abingdon Press, 1992. This book is designed to reflect on life issues facing youth within a small group setting (such as youth group or cabin group).

MacKay, Joy. *Raindrops Keep Falling on my Tent*. American Camping Association, 1981. Activities designed for rainy days including ideas for individuals, cabin groups, and all-camp activities.

Milford, Susan. *The Kid's Nature Book: 365 Indoor/Outdoor Activities and Experiences*. Vermont: Williamson Publishing, 1989.

Maton, Tom. *Rejoice with Creation*. John Knox Press. Exploring summer camp as part of the church's total educational ministry.

Pollack, Shirley. *Building Teen Excitement.* Nashville: Abingdon Press, 1978. This is a resource for leaders of teens. It includes material on group dynamics, programming resources, and projects for youth.

Schmidt, Ernest F. *Woodsmoke and Campfire.* American Camping Association, 1980.

Stock, Gregory. *The Kid's Book of Questions.* New York: Workman Publishing, 1988.

Taylor, Denise David and Taylor, Lawrence, eds. *Awesome Possibilities.* Edmonton: Program Resources Committee of Alberta and Northwest Conference, The United Church of Canada, 1986. This packet contains specially prepared, ready-to-use programs that require little or no preparation. The ideas have been tested out by youth leaders from across the Conference.

Wyatt, Valerie. *Weatherwatch.* Toronto: Kids Can Press, 1990. Facts and projects to help children learn about the weather.

DRAMA

Miller, Joe. T. *The Popcorn Connection.* Contemporary Drama, 1985. Skits dealing with faith in God, nuclear war, intolerance, and more. Available from Contemporary Drama, 885 Elkton Drive, Colorado Springs, CO, 80907, USA. They publish high quality drama and media resources.

Rice, Wayne and Mike Yaconelli. *The Greatest Skits on Earth, Vols. 1, 2, & 3.* Youth Specialties, 1986. Great skits for group use. This is available from Youth Specialties, 1224 Greenfield Drive, El Cajon, CA, 92021, USA. Youth Specialties puts out *Youthworker Journal* and other resources.

Shaffer, Floyd. *Clown Ministry.* Group, 1984. Great ideas for skits and worship and includes information to help prepare costume design and makeup.

Smith, Judy Gattis. *Teaching to Wonder: Spiritual Growth Through Imagination and Movement.* Nashville: Abingdon Press, 1989.

Toomey, Susie Kelly. *Mime Ministry*. Colorado Springs: Meriwether Publishing Ltd, 1986.

Winslow, Barbara. *Spotlight on Drama*. American Camping Association, 1980. A do-it-yourself handbook for a camp drama group.

GAMES

Boyd, Neva L. *The Handbook of Recreational Games*. Dover Publications Inc. 1975.

Boy Scouts of Canada. *Fun Tested Games from A to Z*. Ottawa, ON: Boy Scouts of Canada, 1989.

Campbell, W. *Fun Around the Parachute*. Pointe Claire, QC: Aqua-Percept Inc, 1985.

Fluegalman, Andrew. *The New Games Book*. New York: Dolphin Books, 1976.

Harris, Frank W. *Games, New Expanded Edition*. New York: Frank W. Harris, 1983.

LeFerre, Dale N. *New Games for the Whole Family*. New York: Perigee, 1988. A collection of cooperative games for youth including intergenerational activities.

Orlick, Terry. *The Second Cooperative Sports and Games Book: Over 200 Brand New Noncompetitive Games for Kids and Adults Both*. New York: Pantheon Books, 1982.

Pearse, Jack, Jane McCutcheon and Barrie Laughton. *Clouds on the Clothesline (And 200 Other Great Games)*. Camp Towingo Publications, 1981, 1995. An anthology of camp games: active relays, active games, semi-active relays and games, mixers, musical games, quizzes and quiet games. Available through the Canadian Camping Association, Suite 2, 1806 Avenue Road, Toronto, ON, M5M 3Z1.

Arts and Crafts

Griggs, Patricia. *Creative Activities in Church Education*. Nashville: Abingdon Press, 1987.

Ickis, Marquerite and Reba S. Esh. *The Book of Arts and Crafts*. Dover Publications Inc. 1965.

Rader, Jennifer. *The Rainy Day Activity Book*. New York: Doubleday Books, 1995. Recipes for rainy day projects such as finger paints, play clays, bubbles, sticky stuff, and much, much more. And as an added bonus, the book comes with a bubble blower!

Rogovin, Anne. *Let Me Do It! More than 300 delightful, sensible activities and projects for EVERY child*. Nashville: Abingdon Press, 1990.

National Camping Groups and Related Organizations

Canadian Camping Association
Suite 2, 1806 Avenue Road
Toronto, ON
M5M 3Z1
416-781-4717; fax 416-781-7875

American Camping Association
Publications: Bradford Woods
5000 SR 67N
Martinsville, IN
USA 46151-7902
765-342-8456

Committee on Outdoor Ministry
Program Committee on Ministries in Christian Education
National Council of the Churches of Christ in the USA
475 Riverside Drive, Room 708
New York, NY 10017

(An ecumenical committee that addresses camping trends for outdoor ministry and coordinates the work of the NCCC and curriculum resources.)

NOTES

NOTES

NOTES

NOTES